A WORLD BANK RESEARCH PUBLICATION

Economic Analysis
of Projects

WORLD BANK COUNTRY ECONOMIC REPORTS
WORLD BANK RESEARCH PUBLICATIONS
WORLD BANK STAFF OCCASIONAL PAPERS

Economic Analysis of Projects

LYN SQUIRE
HERMAN G. VAN DER TAK

Published for the World Bank

THE JOHNS HOPKINS UNIVERSITY PRESS
Baltimore and London

THE INTERNATIONAL BANK FOR RECONSTRUCTION AND DEVELOPMENT
1818 H STREET, N.W., WASHINGTON, D.C. 20433, U.S.A.

Originally published, 1975

Paperback edition, 1975
Second printing, 1976

Library of Congress Cataloging in Publication Data

Squire, Lyn, 1946–
    Economic analysis of projects.

    Bibliography: p. 151
    1. Cost effectiveness. 2. Expenditures, Public.
I. van der Tak, Herman G., joint author.
II. International Bank for Reconstruction and
Development. III. Title.
HD47.S67   658.1'552   75–40228
ISBN 0–8018–1817–6
ISBN 0–8018–1818–4 pbk.

Table of Contents

TABLES

Acknowledgments

Many people have contributed to this book. Beyond our considerable intellectual debt to the authors of the major works cited in the "Introduction," we wish to acknowledge the many helpful comments and criticisms we have received from our colleagues both inside and outside the World Bank and from three anonymous reviewers. Although we have benefited greatly from discussions with many people, we owe a special debt to Bela Balassa and Maurice Scott for their sustained interest and searching reviews of successive drafts. Our colleague Johannes Linn helped us generously with his preliminary case studies, especially in clarifying the practical problems of estimating shadow prices. As successive drafts were developed, Lillian Berger, Marta Miro, Aludia Oropesa, and Janette Owens displayed a cheerful forbearance as they *patience* produced efficient transcriptions of illegible copy and incomprehensible symbols. The final manuscript was edited by Goddard W. Winterbottom, and Rachel C. Anderson supervised the processing of proofs. As always, of course, we alone are responsible for any remaining errors of omission and commission.

LYN SQUIRE
HERMAN G. VAN DER TAK

Washington, D.C.
Summer 1975

Economic Analysis
of Projects

Introduction

THIS BOOK SETS FORTH the general approach to the economic analysis of development projects that we recommend for use within the World Bank and other agencies, national and international, that are engaged in project appraisal. Its origin lay in a modest attempt to provide a more satisfactory account of, and rationale for, the Bank's appraisal practices than has obtained heretofore—an attempt that has led to a reconsideration of these practices and an effort to reconcile them, as they have evolved over time, with recent advances in the theoretical literature.[1]

The methodology outlined here deviates in some essential respects from traditional analytical practice. In particular, we recommend a more systematic and consistent estimation and application of shadow prices than has been done in the past, and—again, in contrast to past practice—we favor the calculation of rates of return that take explicit account of the impact of the project on the distribution of income both between investment and consumption and between rich and poor. Although our recommendations do not at this time represent established World Bank practice, the Bank is conducting serious experiments in this area, and its appraisal practices are moving in the general direction advocated in this book. The book therefore is offered as a contribution to the literature on project analysis rather than as an official statement of World Bank policy.

1. The major landmarks that have guided the present book are Organization for Economic Cooperation and Development, *Manual of Industrial Project Analysis* (Paris: OECD, 1969); United Nations Industrial Development Organization, *Guidelines for Project Evaluation* (New York: United Nations, 1972); and I. M. D. Little and J. A. Mirrlees, *Project Appraisal and Planning for Developing Countries* (London: Heinemann Educational Books, 1974). Although these books differ in both emphasis and format, the general thrust of each is such that they may be regarded as a consistent body of literature on project evaluation. □

NATURE OF PROJECT ANALYSIS

The basic economic problem facing all countries is that of allocating inherently limited resources (such as labor, capital, land, and other natural resources, as well as foreign exchange) to a variety of different uses (such as current production of consumer goods and public services as against investment in infrastructure, industry, agriculture, or other sectors of the economy) in such a way that the net benefit to society is as large as possible. Given the limitation of resources, choices must be made among the competing uses, and project analysis is one method of evaluating alternatives in a convenient and comprehensible fashion. In essence, project analysis assesses the benefits and costs of a project and reduces them to a common yardstick. If benefits exceed costs, with both measured by the common yardstick, the project is acceptable; if not, the project should be rejected.

In assessing the merits of different projects, the objectives of any particular society clearly must be taken into account. That is, project costs and benefits must be measured against the extent to which they detract from, or contribute to, achievement of that society's objectives. At a general level, nearly all countries may be assumed to have two primary and simultaneous—if not always equally valued—objectives: to increase total national income, the growth objective, and to improve the distribution of national income, the equity objective. In general, therefore, projects should be assessed in relation to their net contribution to both of these objectives, but this has not always been the practice of the World Bank or of other lending institutions.

TRADITIONAL PRACTICE

Until recently, traditional methods of appraisal have emphasized the growth objective, often to the detriment, if not the virtual exclusion, of the equity objective. This has been justified on the grounds that governments have available to them a diversity of fiscal devices that can be used to redistribute project-generated income in any desired direction. It was argued that project analysis need consider only the growth objective, since this would ensure that the available resources yielded the maximum increment in total national income; the equity objective could then be served by a program of taxes or subsidies that would bring about the desired redistribution of that maximum increment in national income.

At the practical level, the policy concern with growth was interpreted to mean that projects should be selected in the light of their contribution to the maximization of total undifferentiated national income. This appears at first blush to be a faithful interpretation of the policymaker's concern with growth, but it is strictly correct only if it can be assumed that at the margin all units of project-generated income—whether accruing in the form of investment or consumption—make the same contribution to growth. This assumption was generally accepted, either explicitly or implicitly, in traditional practice, as well as in most of the earlier theoretical literature on project analysis. As a result, when theorists attempted to derive, and practitioners to estimate, shadow prices that would reflect the true value of inputs and outputs to society better than market prices, they assumed that at the margin all units of income were equally valuable from the growth point of view and ignored the equity objective. Such shadow prices are here referred to as "efficiency prices."

RECENT INNOVATION

More recently, however, it has been argued that the operational assumption that all units of income make the same contribution to growth may be untenable. For example, in an economy in which the level of national investment is below what is required to secure the desired level of growth, investment may be considered more valuable than consumption. If this argument is accepted, the successful pursuit of the growth objective requires that the distributional effect of the project on consumption and investment be included in the overall assessment of the project's worth, and that project-generated income that leads to investment be assigned a higher value than that which leads to consumption. In this fashion, use of investment resources will be biased in favor of projects that generate more investment, thereby raising national investment toward the desired level.

The validity of this new argument turns on the extent to which the government is free to determine the desired level of investment by means of the traditional instruments of fiscal and monetary policy. Clearly, if the government controls the level of investment in such a manner that at the margin society is indifferent between a unit of investment and a unit of consumption—that is, a unit of either would make the same contribution to welfare—there is no need to differentiate between project-generated income that accrues in the form of investment and in the form of consumption. It can be argued, however, that there is a diversity of social, administrative, and political constraints, especially in developing countries, that may inherently limit the government's ability to increase savings by means of monetary and fiscal policy.

And if these tools of general economic policy cannot successfully break the diverse constraints, other policy instruments, including the selection of projects, can and perhaps should be used to achieve the desired goal.

Theorists and practitioners therefore turned their attention to the derivation and estimation of shadow prices that recognized a suboptimal rate of investment. But once there was a recognition of the constraints on the government's ability to secure the desired distribution of income between investment and consumption, it was but a short step to the realization that the separation of the growth and equity objectives may not be justified: that is, that the government's ability to redistribute income in general may be limited. On this basis it was concluded that project analysts should investigate the impact of projects not only on the distribution of income between consumption and investment but also on the distribution of income between the rich and the poor. Shadow prices that include both these distributional aspects are here described as "social prices."

This book may be viewed in part as an attempt to provide an up-to-date statement of these ideas and to summarize the main developments in the recent literature as they relate to the traditional practice of the World Bank and other lending institutions. In particular, it is shown that the traditional method of project analysis represents a special case of the more general method recommended here. The text attempts to clarify the conditions under which the traditional method is appropriate and to define more clearly the nature of some efficiency prices (for example, the shadow exchange rate) and how they can be estimated. This part of the discussion, however, does not basically alter the standard practice followed thus far with respect to calculations of shadow prices and rates of return; it seeks simply to systematize existing practice into a more consistent methodology.

In addition, and perhaps more important, the book seeks to provide more specific guidance than is available elsewhere on the mechanics of incorporating considerations of income distribution into the traditional calculation of rates of return. Basically, this involves attaching suitable weights, to be determined by the appropriate decisionmaker, to the benefits from the project that accrue in different forms (consumption or investment) and to different beneficiaries (rich or poor). Such weights might be assigned directly or, as described in the text, they may be derived from underlying notions of a welfare function. The most important issue, however, is not the technique for deriving the weights, which will undoubtedly be refined in due course; it is that, whatever weights are considered to reflect properly the relative value attached to benefits for various higher or lower income groups and to additional investment, these weights be consistently and systematically applied when evaluating the socioeconomic merits of a project. Only in this way will it be possible to allow in project decisions for the tradeoff between raising consumption levels of the poor and accelerating overall economic growth. Project evaluation procedures that neglect these aspects in their decisionmaking criterion are not responsive to recent concern with the distribution of the benefits of economic growth or to earlier concern with the achievement of growth. Evaluation procedures employed by the World Bank and other agencies, including national governments, should be consistent with general policy on these matters. This means, for the Bank and other external agencies, that the appropriate set of weights for project analysis must be worked out in cooperation with the client countries.

POSSIBLE OBJECTIONS

Although the method outlined in this book has been widely accepted as, in principle, an important step forward in improving appraisal techniques and practices, doubts have been expressed with regard to (a) some aspects of the methodology, in particular, its appearance of spurious accuracy and dependence on dubious assumptions; (b) the possible lowering of rigorous appraisal standards; (c) its practical significance for project decisions; (d) its feasibility in regular operations of the World Bank and other agencies; and (e) its desirability, in view of the expected costs and benefits of the proposed approach. These objections and related issues are discussed below.

There is, of course, ample scope for further improving the methodology set forth in this book. The techniques for deriving and estimating shadow prices will undoubtedly evolve with further practical experience. Some elements of the analysis, particularly with respect to the distributional impact, are necessarily rather crude. In all cases, though, it is important, first, that all major considerations such as income distribution and fiscal constraints be included in the analysis (although in a crude fashion); and, second, that shortcuts such as those discussed in the text be adopted in full awareness of the approximation involved and the conditions in which they are justified.

The reader should not be misled by the apparent accuracy of the methodology. The equations describe concretely the specific relations underlying the analysis. They make clear what considerations were taken into account and what assumptions were made. This should not be taken to imply, however, that the postulated relations are accurate in the sense of providing a complete picture of reality. They are thought to give a good representation of the more significant features that should be taken into account in many cases, but, as the text tries to make clear, other factors and other relations may give a better approximation in some cases. Because both the nature of the relations among key factors and the magnitude of the parameters governing these relations are subject to substantial uncertainty, we do not claim great accuracy for the proposed method of analysis. At the same time, the cost estimates, demand projections, and price forecasts that are included in more conventional cost-benefit analysis are also beset by a large margin of error. The real point is not the degree of accuracy but the taking into account of all major factors bearing on a project decision as best one can rather than simply ignoring them.

Again, the simple welfare function that provides the central theme of the discussion of distributional aspects of project analysis can easily be criticized as oversimplistic. Others may prefer more complex functions that allow for a greater range and variety of judgments on equity and social justice. We believe, however, that many basic features of distributional problems can be satisfactorily clarified and reflected in project analysis by the simple welfare function used. Furthermore, more complex functions are likely to cause even greater problems of estimation.

The use of distribution weights to determine the social return on projects does not mean that appraisal standards would be lowered. On the contrary, the methodology outlined in this book involves a more rigorous and systematic analysis than normally is carried out. The criterion for acceptability of a project is changed, but it is not more lenient. Some projects that otherwise would have been rejected will be acceptable because their distributional effects are given weight in the criterion; some otherwise acceptable projects will be rejected because of an adverse distributional impact.

Nor does the criterion neglect growth: the weight assigned to investment (and hence growth) is always positive and is determined jointly, on the basis of the same welfare function, with the weights attaching to benefits to richer and poorer people. Society's concern with growth can therefore be balanced against its concern with current consumption and equity in such a manner that neither concern is neglected.

The recommended approach should be more rigorous than current practice in another respect: it envisages a more systematic assessment and a more consistent application of the traditional efficiency prices, as well as of the recommended social prices incorporating distribution weights, than is customary in traditional analysis. With respect to both efficiency and social prices, it is important that public agencies, national or international, use the same estimates in the analysis of all projects in a particular country in order to provide greater assurance that shadow prices are estimated and applied in an objective and unbiased manner. This need for consistent use of shadow prices applies to all stages in the analysis of investment choices up to the final decision to proceed with the project.

In general, the significance of the proposed method of analysis is that it produces a systematic bias in project decisions favoring projects that benefit the poor rather than the rich and that result in higher savings and further growth rather than higher current consumption. Such an outcome represents not a distortion but is as it should be, since the extent of these biases is determined by the distributional weights, which are set in such a way that they reflect the fundamental socioeconomic objectives of the particular society. As a result, projects will tend to be selected or rejected with due regard to their impact on income distribution and growth. Although these factors may or may not be decisive for any particular project choice—depending on the distributional effects and the weights given to them—we expect this analysis to result in a pattern of investment that will differ significantly from the pattern that would emerge if distributional considerations were to continue to be ignored.

As in all project appraisal methods, the significance of this new methodology becomes greater the earlier it is applied in the project cycle. This underscores the importance of focusing economic analysis on the project at the time when its design is taking shape and when choices are still open, rather than when the project has become frozen and rejection may be difficult. But this is not an argument for or against any particular method of project analysis, including the one set forth here.

In our judgment the methodology detailed in this book can be implemented without undue difficulty, although ad hoc adjustments may be necessary to accommodate data availability in any particular case. As with project analysis generally, no great accuracy should be expected with respect to the necessary value judgments, but this does not mean that the results are arbitrary. The reliability of the necessary estimates will be improved by systematic cross-checks on the plausibility of the results obtained: we believe that the inevitable margins of error will be no greater than with respect to estimates required for the traditional approach. Although additional time and effort will be required, some of the more time-consuming computations relate to the more careful analysis of efficiency prices (such as the conversion factors corresponding to the traditional shadow exchange rate) rather than to the assessment of distribution weights.

The principal burden of estimating the country parameters will fall on the national planning office or the country desks of international agencies such as the World Bank. A substantial part of this work, however, is necessary also for the preparation of other planning documents and economic reports; in fact, the estimation of shadow prices would provide an important focus for some of this work, the relevance of which could be increased by closer attention to such areas as tariff structure, fiscal constraints, employment policy, and income distribution. The results of this work, if synthesized in country parameters for shadow pricing, would relieve the project analyst of the present need to make ad hoc estimates of, for example, the shadow exchange rate and the shadow rate of interest. For the project analyst, the new methodology implies primarily a greater need to determine the income distribution effects of the project. Although this involves additional work, it is essential for any systematic concern with the distributional effects of projects.

There is little doubt, in our view, that the methodology for project analysis recommended in this book is feasible, but the question remains whether it is desirable, in view of its costs and benefits. As usual in cost-benefit analysis, it is easier to document the costs than the benefits. As argued above, we believe the additional cost—in time and effort—to estimate shadow prices along the lines of this book are relatively small, since most of the work is required for other purposes as well—and, in particular, the introduction of distribution weights accounts for a small fraction of the work involved. Nevertheless, the initial cost of transition to the new methodology is substantial, since users must become familiar with the new techniques, and initial estimates of country parameters for shadow-pricing must be built up.

The benefits of the proposed methodology are implicit in the earlier discussions. Estimates of efficiency prices, as well as shadow prices incorporating distributional weights, will be derived more carefully and used more systematically than under the ad hoc procedures that now form common practice. Taking account of essential considerations relating to the distribution of benefits and fiscal constraints and savings, even if necessarily in a crude manner, can only improve the quality of project decisions.

TOWARD IMPLEMENTATION

The new methodology cannot, of course, be adopted overnight for the analysis of all projects in all countries. Time will be required for staff to become familiar with various aspects of its general framework, the various approaches suggested for estimating shadow prices, and the interpretation of the results. Project analysis in accord with the new method can be undertaken only after country parameters for shadow-pricing have been estimated; for an agency concerned with a large number of countries, this obviously can be accomplished only over a period of time. This introduction only gradually over a period of a few years can also result in further fine tuning of the specific suggestions made in this book.

As part of this implementation phase, the World Bank is gradually introducing consistent and systematic use of efficiency prices into its regular operational work, along the lines sketched out in this book. The practicality of systematic use of social prices incorporating distributional aspects is being tested on an experimental basis in the appraisal of a limited number of projects in selected countries. A series of case studies is being conducted to heighten the Bank's perception of the difficulties and advantages of the proposed methodology and to advance appreciation of when and where shortcuts may be appropriate. Thus far, these studies have estimated shadow prices for nine countries, and steps are being taken to apply them in about twenty projects. Some of these studies, it is hoped, will be published in a subsequent volume, together with the main results of the implementation exercise.

Therefore, as noted earlier, the methodology outlined in this book does not constitute World Bank policy at this time but only a direction in which the Bank is moving and conducting serious experimentation.

ORGANIZATION OF THE BOOK

The book consists of three major parts. The first provides a broad nontechnical review of the basic notions of cost-benefit analysis. The second gives a self-contained explanation of the nature of shadow prices and how they can be derived, in principle, so as to reflect appropriately a wide range of economic conditions and value judgments concerning basic policy objectives pertaining to growth and distribution. The third reviews various approximate methods that may be feasible and appropriate for estimating these shadow prices in practice, depending on data availability and circumstances in a particular country. A technical appendix contains a more rigorous derivation of some of the formulas that are merely discussed in the main text.

Throughout the discussion the perspective is economic and not financial or technical. The approach followed reflects the evolution of Bank appraisal methods, as well as advances in analytical techniques that have been made over the last decade. Although this book provides guidelines dealing with a wide range of problems, it does not try to provide an exhaustive treatment of the subject. In particular, it does not deal with sector-specific issues, nor does it contain cookbook-style instructions for the many different situations the analyst will confront in practice. Instead, we have concentrated on providing broad understanding and general guidelines that we hope will enable the analyst to make sensible adaptations to the specific circumstances of each case. The guidelines are intended to be guidelines only; they are not meant to substitute for good judgment on the part of the analyst.

An effort has been made to make the subject accessible to a wide audience and to combine conciseness and clarity of exposition. The issues dealt with, however, are intrinsically complex and require a modicum of economic understanding. Some sections are probably easier than others, and the various parts are addressed to somewhat different readers. The first part, on basic notions of cost-benefit analysis, should give a good general idea of the underlying rationale and purpose of the analysis and be accessible to a wide range of nontechnical readers. The later parts, on the derivation and estimation of shadow prices, tend to be more technical. Depending on their familiarity with economics in general and cost-benefit analysis in particular, readers may well complain that the treatment of some topics and in some sections is too long or too brief, overcomplicated or oversimplified, excessively technical or insufficiently rigorous. We like to think that this is inevitable, given our intention to reach a rather heterogeneous group of readers.

□

PART I

Basic Notions of Cost-Benefit Analysis

THIS OPENING PART CONTAINS a general account of the basic practices recommended by the authors for use by the World Bank and other agencies in analyzing the economic merit of development projects. The following relatively nontechnical discussion covers the nature and principal features of this analysis, and of the problems that often arise. Although this review provides guidelines for responding to certain of these problems, is is not an exhaustive treatment of all aspects of project analysis, and should be supplemented by more extensive and detailed discussion of various issues that are touched on only briefly in this book.[1]

Chapter one contains a discussion in broad terms of the basic ideas behind cost-benefit analysis and of some of the concepts that will be developed later. The types of costs and benefits of projects that are relevant in their economic appraisal are identified in chapter two, while in chapter three consideration is given in general qualitative terms to how such costs and benefits should be valued and in what circumstances shadow prices will be appropriate. Chapter four contains a demonstration of how costs and benefits may be compared so that a meaningful decision can be made about the value of the project to the country. Finally, methods for taking into account the considerable risk elements and uncertainties that are commonly involved in undertaking a project are examined in chapter five.

A general warning is in order at the outset. The discussion of cost-benefit analysis in part I pays considerable attention to the concept of shadow prices, and parts II and III are fully devoted to shadow price issues. This emphasis reflects the crucial role of shadow prices in measuring the contribution of a project to a country's socioeconomic

---

1. See the bibliography, in which references are arranged by subject. □

development objectives. Such extensive treatment is certainly not a measure of the time spent on questions of shadow prices in actual project analysis or of their importance relative to other project problems. Judicious use of shadow prices is an important means for assessing the economic merits of a project to a country, but it is not a substitute for careful analysis of its technical features, investment and operating costs, organizational arrangements, market prospects, financial results, and many other considerations relevant to the outcome of a project. These basic dimensions of project analysis are largely taken for granted in this book.

CHAPTER ONE

The Context of Project Analysis

ALL COUNTRIES, but particularly the developing countries, are faced with the basic economic problem of allocating limited resources such as labor at all levels of skill, management and administrative capacity, capital, land and other natural resources, and foreign exchange, to many different uses such as current production of consumer goods and public services or investment in infrastructure, industry, agriculture, education, and other sectors. These different uses of resources, however, are not the final aim of the allocative process; rather, they are the means by which an economy can marshal its resources in the pursuit of more fundamental objectives such as the removal of poverty, the promotion of growth, and the reduction of inequalities in income. Using limited resources in one direction (for example, investment in industry) reduces the resources available for use in another direction (investment in agriculture). Pursuit of one objective (better income distribution) may involve a sacrifice in other objectives (rapid growth).

Thus, there are clearly tradeoffs: a country can have more of some things and less of others, but not more of everything at once. A choice therefore has to be made among competing uses of resources based on the extent to which they help the country achieve its fundamental objectives. If a country consistently chooses allocations of resources that achieve most in terms of these objectives, it ensures that its limited resources are put to their best possible use.

Project analysis is a method of presenting this choice between competing uses of resources in a convenient and comprehensible fashion. In essence, project analysis assesses the benefits and costs of a project and reduces them to a common denominator. If benefits exceed costs—both expressed in terms of this common denominator—the project is acceptable: if not, the project should be rejected. As such, project analysis may appear divorced from both the fundamental objectives of the economy and the possible alternative uses of resources in other projects. The definition of benefits and costs, however, is such that these factors play an integral part in the decision to accept or reject. Benefits are defined relative to their effect on the fundamental objectives; costs are defined relative to their opportunity cost, which is the benefit for-

[15]

gone by not using these resources in the best of the available alternative investments that cannot be undertaken if the resources are used in the project. The forgone benefits are in turn defined relative to their effect on the fundamental objectives. By defining costs and benefits in this fashion we try to ensure that acceptance of a project implies that no alternative use of the resources consumed by this project would secure a better result from the perspective of the country's objectives.

Economic analysis of projects is similar in form to financial analysis in that both assess the profit of an investment. The concept of financial profit, however, is not the same as the social profit of economic analysis. The financial analysis of a project identifies the money profit accruing to the project-operating entity, whereas social profit measures the effect of the project on the fundamental objectives of the whole economy. These different concepts of profit are reflected in the different items considered to be costs and benefits and in their valuation.[1] Thus, a money payment made by the project-operating entity for, say, wages is by definition a financial cost. But it will be an economic cost only to the extent that the use of labor in this project implies some sacrifice elsewhere in the economy with respect to output and other objectives of the country. Conversely, if the project has an economic cost in this sense that does not involve a corresponding money outflow from the project entity—for example, because of environmental effects or subsidies—this cost is not a financial cost. The two types of cost need not coincide. Economic costs may be larger or smaller than financial costs. Similar comments apply to economic and financial benefits. Economic costs and benefits are measured by "shadow prices," which may well differ from the market prices appropriate for financial costs and benefits.

Shadow prices are determined by the interaction of the fundamental policy objectives and the basic resource availabilities. If a particular resource is very scarce (that is, many alternative uses are competing for that resource), then its shadow price, or opportunity cost (the forgone benefit in the best available alternative that must be sacrificed), will tend to be high. If the supply of this resource were greater, however, the demand arising from the next best uses could be satisfied in decreasing order of importance, and its opportunity cost (or shadow price) would fall. Market prices will often reflect this scarcity correctly, but there is good reason to believe that in less developed countries imperfect markets may cause a divergence between market and shadow prices. Such

1. The definition of "financial analysis" used here represents only one of several concepts of financial analysis, all of which have their specific purposes. □

divergences are thought to be particularly severe in the markets for three important resources: labor, capital, and foreign exchange. Chapter three is concerned largely with the appropriate shadow-pricing of these resources.

Resource availabilities, however, need not be the only constraints operating in the economy: political and social constraints may be equally binding. The alternatives open to the government in pursuing its development objectives can be limited by these noneconomic constraints to a narrower range than that implied by the basic resource availabilities. If the tools of general economic policy—that is, fiscal and monetary policy—cannot break these constraints, project analysis should take account of them by means of appropriate adjustments in shadow prices. For example, if the government is unable to secure a desired redistribution of income through taxation, it can use the allocation of investment resources as an alternative method of redistributing income. If in project analysis higher values were to be attached to increases in income accruing to the poorer groups within society, investment would be biased in favor of these groups. In other words, all available policy tools should be working jointly toward the same goals. If one instrument is inoperative or blunted, other instruments may be used to achieve the same end.

Project analysis is designed to permit project-by-project decision-making on the appropriate choices between competing uses of resources, with costs and benefits being defined and valued, in principle, so as to measure their impact on the development objectives of the country. In many cases, however, a more direct link is necessary with the sector and economy as a whole: for example, the merit of a project characterized by economies of scale cannot be judged without making an estimate of the demand for its output, and this in turn requires placing the project in its sectoral and country context.

Furthermore, in practice, many shadow prices (for land and natural resources, for example) are difficult to determine independent of the project appraisal process, because they depend on the alternative projects that have been rejected. This is the basic reason why a systematic scrutiny of plausible alternatives is at the heart of the appraisal process: it is not sufficient in practice to select an acceptable project whose benefits appear to exceed costs; it is necessary to search for alternatives with a larger surplus of benefits over identified costs. If such projects are found, it means that the opportunity cost of using, say, land in the project originally considered acceptable has been underestimated or wholly neglected.

Consideration of alternatives is the single most important feature of proper project analysis throughout the project cycle, from the development plan for the particular sector through identification to appraisal. Many of the more important choices are made at early stages when decisions are made concerning the alternatives that are to be rejected or retained for further, more detailed study. If economic analysis is to make a maximum contribution to the attempt to ensure that scarce resources are used to best advantage for the country, it should be used from the earliest phases of this process of successive sifting and narrowing down of options that are open to the country. The use of shadow prices reflecting basic policy objectives and resource constraints only in the final stage of appraisal, when most of the essential choices with respect to types of project and project design have already been made, tends to be mainly cosmetic. To be an effective aid in decisionmaking, shadow prices should also be used in framing sector strategies and in identifying promising project possibilities and designing their major features.   □

CHAPTER TWO

Identifying Relevant Costs and Benefits

WHATEVER THE NATURE OF THE PROJECT, its implementation will always reduce the supply of inputs ("consumed" by the project) and increase the supply of outputs ("produced" by the project). Without the project, the supply of these inputs and outputs to the rest of the economy would have been different. Examining this difference between the availabilities of inputs and outputs with and without the project is the basic method of identifying its costs and benefits. In many cases the situation without the project is not simply a continuation of the status quo, but rather the situation that is expected to exist if the project is not undertaken, because some increases in output and costs are often expected to occur anyway. Furthermore, some projects, such as those involving modernization and land conservation, have as their primary aim the prevention of future cost increases or benefit decreases. The without situation must then include these cost increases or benefit decreases in order to fully reflect the improvement engendered by the project. Thus, an accurate description of the situation without, as of that with, the project may involve difficult judgments; it does not normally correspond to the situation "before" and "after."

The projected financial statement of the project entity will often be a good starting place for identifying economic costs and benefits. In general, two types of adjustment must be made to the financial calculation so that it can reflect economic concepts: first, it may be necessary to include (exclude) some costs and benefits which have been excluded from (included in) the financial analysis; and, second, some inputs and outputs may have to be revalued if their shadow and market prices differ. Only the first adjustment is considered here; the second is the subject matter of chapter three.

TRANSFER PAYMENTS

Some payments that appear in the cost streams of the financial analysis do not represent direct claims on the country's resources but merely reflect a transfer of the control over resource allocation from one member or sector of society to another. For example, the payment of interest by the project entity on a domestic loan merely transfers purchasing power from the project entity to the lender. The purchasing power of the interest payment does reflect control over resources, but its transfer does not use up real resources and to that extent is not an economic cost. Similarly, the loan itself and its repayment are financial transfers. The investment, however, or other expenditure that the loan finances involves real economic costs. The financial cost of the loan occurs when the loan is repaid, but the economic cost occurs when the loan is spent.[1] The economic analysis does not, in general, need to concern itself with the financing of the investment: that is, with the sources of funds and how they are repaid. Again, depreciation allowances may not correspond to actual use of resources, and should therefore be excluded from the cost stream. The economic cost of using an asset is fully reflected in the initial investment cost less its discounted terminal value. Finally, taxes and subsidies are also transfer payments and as such do not constitute a resource cost.

The preceding rule is subject to one important exception. Although transfer payments such as taxes and interest are not a resource cost, they do have an impact on the distribution of income and possibly on savings. And if the government wishes to use project selection as a means of improving income distribution or increasing savings, then this should be taken into account when determining the costs and benefits of a project and should be reflected in the shadow prices of factor inputs and incomes.

CONTINGENCIES

Contingency allowances are determined by engineering and financial considerations that are beyond the scope of this book, but it is important to examine the treatment of contingency allowances in the economic appraisal. To the extent that the physical contingency allowance is a part of the expected value of the project's costs, it should be included in the economic analysis. Any allowance beyond this should be excluded from the basic data but should be examined in the sensitivity or risk analysis. The project evaluator will require the assistance of an engineer in determining the nature of physical contingency allowances.

1. These points also apply to foreign loans unless the loan is tied to the project (that is, would not be available for any other project), in which case its economic cost is the stream of associated repayments. World Bank loans are not considered tied. A country, however, should not borrow beyond the point at which the real cost of the debt service exceeds the return on the marginal project. □

To the extent that the price contingency covers expected increases in relative prices of project items, it should be included in the economic analysis. Any price contingency for domestic and foreign inflation of the general price level should be excluded—provided that differential rates of inflation in supplier countries are offset by currency realignments. If such realignment does not occur, the part of the price contingency covering excess inflation—inflation beyond that in the currency used as common denominator—should be included in the economic analysis.

SUNK COSTS

Sunk costs are defined as those costs which have been incurred on the project before appraisal and which therefore cannot be avoided even if they are considered utterly wasteful. They should, of course, be excluded from the cost of the project for the purpose of deciding whether to proceed with the project: bygones are bygones, and only costs that can still be avoided matter in this regard. For example, the economic merit of a project designed to complete another project that was started earlier and left unfinished does not depend on the costs already incurred but only on the costs of completion. (Similarly, the benefits from the new project are only those which will arise over and above those which may flow from the earlier, uncompleted work.) This treatment of sunk costs may result in a high return on the investment in completing the project, but this reflects the nature of the decision being made. In addition to this calculation of the return on the incremental investment, it is usually desirable to show the return on the total project, including sunk costs, to throw light on the question of whether, in hindsight, the original decision to proceed with the project was well founded.

EXTERNALITIES AND LINKAGES

Certain effects of the project do not impose a cost or confer a benefit within the confines of the project itself. But if these effects, known as externalities, affect the achievement of the country's objectives (either positively or negatively), they should be included in the economic analysis. Unfortunately, externalities are sometimes difficult to identify and nearly always difficult to measure.

On the benefit side, demonstration and training effects are often cited as externalities, but these are not amenable to quantification at present. Various forms of pollution and congestion, use of water that affects yields of wells elsewhere, and side effects from irrigation schemes on health or fisheries are among standard examples of external costs; if they are significant and measurable, they should be counted as economic costs. Whether or not externalities can be quantified, they should at least be discussed in qualitative terms.

Price effects caused by the project also are often included in the scope of externalities. The project may lead to higher prices for the inputs that it requires and lower prices for the outputs that it produces. The project may also result in lower demand and prices for competing products or services or higher demand and prices for complementary ones. What are known as "forward linkage effects" thus may occur in industries that use or process a project's output, and backward linkages in industries that supply its inputs, in that such industries are encouraged or stimulated by increased demand and higher prices for their output or lower prices for their inputs. Conversely, other producers may lose because they now face increased competition, and other users of inputs required by the project may have to pay higher prices. The project may have wide-ranging repercussions on demands of inputs and outputs and cause gains and losses for producers and consumers other than those involved in the project itself.

Such external costs and benefits may or may not have to be added to the more direct costs and benefits of the project. The direct social profit is a comprehensive measure of all economic gains and losses of the project—provided that two conditions are met. First, the government should be indifferent as to who gains and who loses as a result of the project. If it attaches different weights to gains and losses depending on the person or region affected, the direct social profit on the output from the project is not a full measure of all its positive and negative effects on the country's socioeconomic objectives. There is then no remedy but to trace as well as possible the repercussions on the rest of the economy. Whether this is a serious qualification in practice depends on the extent to which the project results in price changes. If induced price changes are minor, or if income distribution weights of affected groups are approximately the same, exclusion of such external price effects from the economic analysis of the project may result in a reasonable approximation.

Second, and perhaps more serious, the direct costs and benefits of the project arising from the project's own output and inputs do not provide a complete measure of its social profit in cases in which other producers whose output is affected by the project do not sell in perfect markets in which price is equated with the cost of production at shadow prices (or social marginal cost). In such cases—which are, of course, normal—there will be gains and losses that are not measured by the social profit on direct output from the project. For example, if an improved road diverts traffic from a railway that charges rates below marginal cost, this diversion entails a social gain on reduced rail traffic (because the previous social loss on this traffic is no longer incurred), in addition to the social profit on road traffic as usually measured (by changes in the area between its demand and supply curves). In practice, it is not feasible to trace all externalities arising from such market imperfections: the analyst can only hope to capture the grosser distortions on more immediately affected changes in output.

Externalities of various kinds are thus clearly troublesome, and there is no altogether satisfactory way in which to deal with them. This is no reason simply to ignore them, however; an attempt should always be made to identify them and, if they appear significant, to measure them. In some cases it is helpful to internalize externalities by considering a package of closely related activities as one project. This procedure is also convenient in cases in which externalities, strictly speaking, play no role but in which it is difficult, if not impossible, to estimate demand—and hence the social value of the output from the project—without closely linking it to related activities. A standard example is the analysis of irrigation projects in which benefits are measured relative to agricultural output rather than to water.

MULTIPLIER EFFECTS

In an economy suffering from general excess capacity, project investment may cause a further increase in income as the additional rounds of spending following the investment reduce the excess capacity. General excess capacity, however, is not the situation in which less developed countries typically find themselves. If it were otherwise, development would be a far easier task, and could be furthered simply by spending more. This does not deny the existence of secondary expenditure effects: as will be discussed in chapter three, these effects may be important, and should be measured by examining the pattern of consumption expenditure induced by the project. Different patterns of second-round expenditure out of incomes generated by the project will have different economic consequences: expenditure patterns can be expected to be different for different income classes and for different regions within a country.

INTERNATIONAL EFFECTS

Some external effects of a project may extend beyond the borders of the country concerned. For example, a project's output may increase exports or substitute for imports, thus tending to reduce world prices and thereby benefit other importing countries and harm other exporting countries. Or the increase in demand and possibly prices for inputs into the project may affect other countries, favorably or adversely. Or a project in one country may influence the environment of a neighboring country by, for example, diverting or polluting a river common to both countries.

All such external effects on other countries are similar in nature to the externalities discussed above and raise similar problems. The crucial issue in this case is whether account should be taken of benefits accruing to, or of costs imposed on, other countries—which may be developed countries or other developing countries, which may be poorer or better off than the country concerned, and which may be politically close or otherwise.

This issue clearly depends on value judgments. The traditional policy of the World Bank and most other lending agencies is to take account of physical externalities, as in the case of international rivers, and expect agreement between the countries concerned on the sharing of water and appropriate compensation for any untoward effects. Thus far, however, it has not normally taken into account external price effects on other countries caused by the projects it finances, and, with some exceptions for multinational projects, it evaluates investment projects from the point of view of the country in which the project is to be undertaken. This means that costs borne by foreign countries or foreign participants in the project, as well as benefits accruing to them, are excluded from the economic analysis of the project. Some implications of this are discussed further in chapter three.

DOUBLE COUNTING

All relevant costs and benefits should be included when evaluating a project, but they should not be recorded twice. Such double counting can arise in two ways. First, as noted above, external benefits and costs may be included (erroneously) even though they are already fully accounted for in the social profit measure of the project. For example, increases in agricultural output may mistakenly be claimed as additional benefits of, say, a road project when such benefits are already reflected in the usual measure of the social surplus gained on the transport services to be provided. Second, benefits may be claimed for employment or for foreign exchange earnings, in addition to the estimated social profit of the project. Provided that labor inputs into the project and the project's foreign exchange costs and savings have been evaluated in relation to shadow prices that represent a comprehensive measure of their value to the economy, any such employment or foreign exchange effects have already been taken into account and should not be added as separate benefits. The contributions of increased employment and foreign exchange earnings to the socioeconomic objectives of the government have then been given their full and proper weight in deriving the social surplus of the project. This does not mean that employment and foreign exchange effects should not be discussed further, but it does mean that any discussion must be consistent with the assumptions underlying the economic evaluation of the project. □

CHAPTER THREE

Valuation and Shadow Prices

EVERY PROJECT USES UP resources (inputs) and produces outputs. Those inputs (costs) and outputs (benefits) which are to be included in the economic analysis of the project have been identified in the previous chapter; the values of these costs and benefits to the economy can now be considered. These values depend, of course, on the value judgments by the government, as well as on technical and behavioral parameters and on resource and policy constraints. Value judgments by the government determine the weight to be given to future consumption relative to present consumption: that is, to growth (depending on savings and investments) as against present consumption; to benefits for different classes of income recipients or different regions; to future employment relative to present employment; and to other possible objectives such as national independence or modernization. Policy constraints of an institutional-administrative or a political character can limit the choice of path that the economy can follow in pursuing its development objectives to a narrower range than is imposed by constraints of technical and behavioral parameters and resource availabilities.

Shadow prices are here defined as the value of the contribution to the country's basic socioeconomic objectives made by any marginal change in the availability of commodities or factors of production. Thus, shadow prices will depend on both the fundamental objectives of the country and the economic environment in which the marginal changes occur. The economic environment typically will be determined by the physical constraints on resources and by various constraints that limit the government's control over economic development. Any changes in objectives or constraints will therefore necessitate a change in the estimated shadow prices.

Two points should be made about this definition of shadow prices. First, these prices relate to an economic environment in which distortions may be expected to persist: they are not the equilibrium prices that would prevail in a distortion-free economy. This should not be interpreted, however, as a passive acceptance of existing distortions; in fact, the estimation of (second-best) shadow prices supplies important information that can be used as a basis for designing policies to remove the distortions. Second, those conducting the economic analysis should have a clear definition of the socioeconomic goals of the government's development policy. If an international agency such as the World Bank conducts the analysis, it must try to arrive at an understanding with the government about these goals before the analysis is undertaken. If views diverge—with respect to the desired distribution of the gains from development, for example—the agency should analyze the proposed project relative to both its objectives and those of the government and satisfy itself that the project meets the objectives of both.

SHADOW RATE OF INTEREST

In shaping its investment and fiscal policies the government will have to choose between encouraging savings and investment and thus future growth and immediate increases in consumption and living standards. The government—in the absence of policy constraints arising from political feasibility, administrative costs, and repercussions on incentives—could ensure through its fiscal policy that at the margin additional savings to promote growth and future consumption are in its view as valuable as additional present consumption. In that case project analysis need not concern itself with the impact of a project on consumption or savings, but should concentrate on the impact on income, irrespective of its use for consumption or savings, since both are worth the same. There is in that case no need to distinguish between savings and consumption when assessing costs and benefits.

In some cases, however, the government might prefer more rapid growth and higher savings and investments at the expense of current consumption, but it sees as insurmountable various administrative and political obstacles to effecting the necessary fiscal measures. Savings are then at a premium—or, equivalently, consumption is at a discount. This has implications for the discount rate that is appropriate for making benefits and costs in future years commensurate with those occurring now. If consumption is used as the common yardstick for measuring consumption and savings—that is, as the "numéraire"—the appropriate discount rate is the "consumption rate of interest," which measures the discount attached to having additional consumption next year rather than this year. But if savings are used as the numéraire, the appropriate discount rate should measure the decline in value of savings that accrue in successive periods. More generally, the discount rate is defined as the rate at which the value of the numéraire falls over time.

The approach can be further refined by distinguishing different types of consumption and different types of saving. Thus, the consumption of the rich may be considered less valuable than that of the poor; or public sector saving may be considered more valuable than private sector saving. Such refinements require a careful specification of what is to be used as the numéraire, or common measuring rod, but the principle remains the same as in the savings-consumption case. If a dollar of consumption by the rich is not worth the same as a dollar of consumption by the poor or a dollar of revenue by the government, a common yardstick is needed in which to express the project accounts. The choice of this numéraire does not affect project analysis because the selection of projects depends only on relative prices, whereas the numéraire determines only the absolute price level. But failure to be clear about the numéraire and to use it systematically for expressing all benefits and costs on a common basis can result only in misleading accounts of the project's social profit.

It is recommended that public income be used as the numéraire for measuring costs and benefits in the economic analysis of projects. Two points should be made about this numéraire. First, public income that is not freely available for all uses is not as valuable as income that can be spent for whatever purpose is desired. For example, public income that is earmarked for certain expenditures or accrues in a currency that the government cannot freely convert into other currencies is less valuable than freely available income in fully convertible currency. As long as public income is fully convertible, it does not matter whether it is expressed in a foreign currency or in domestic currency (converted at the official rates of exchange). The use of local currency for this purpose often proves more convenient, and this practice is adopted here. Second, for a numéraire to be a useful yardstick, its value should remain constant over time. Therefore, we define our chosen numéraire as freely available public sector income of constant purchasing power measured in units of local currency.[1]

As noted earlier, the discount rate used in the economic analysis of projects should match the unit of account, or numéraire, in which costs and benefits are measured. The discount rate that we suggest be used in appraisal work, here described as the "accounting rate of interest," should be the rate of fall over time in the value of the numéraire, as defined

---

1. Of course, constant purchasing power can be defined only in relation to a particular bundle of commodities. The bundle chosen and the significance of the choice are discussed further in "Definition of the Numéraire" in chapter seven. □

above: that is, public income measured in the domestic currency equivalent of foreign exchange. This accounting rate of interest is not the same, in general, as the discount rate used in the traditional procedure and that has been interpreted as the opportunity cost of capital: that is, the marginal productivity of additional investment in the best alternative uses.

The precise relation between the opportunity cost of capital, the accounting rate of interest, and the consumption rate of interest is outlined in part II, but it may be noted here that the traditional procedure used by the World Bank and most other project-financing agencies essentially implies a judgment that there is no significant imbalance between the value attached to current consumption and future growth (current savings). In assessing the costs and benefits of a project, appraisal reports that do not differentiate between consumption and savings are implicitly treating both as of equal value. This approach may not always be appropriate. In cases in which growth rates are considered too low because of insufficient savings rather than inefficient use of resources, and greater fiscal efforts are ruled out by overriding constraints, project appraisals should take account of the greater value that then attaches to savings than to consumption. A further breakdown of consumption may be warranted if the government wishes to use project selection to influence the current distribution of consumption. The assumptions employed in such cases should be specified in an agency's appraisal report.[2]

SHADOW WAGE RATES

Similar considerations obtain in examining the issue of the economic cost of employing labor on the project. The appropriate shadow wage rate and the interpretation of what it represents will differ depending on the value judgments and policy constraints that are considered applicable. The value judgments should be consistent with those underlying the estimates of other shadow prices. If, for example, savings and growth are held at a premium, this should be reflected in both the shadow rate of interest (as argued above) and the shadow wage rate. Shadow prices are interdependent: changes in assumptions determining one affect others as well.

In the simplest case, the shadow wage rate aims at measuring nothing more than the opportunity cost of labor: that is, the marginal output of labor forgone elsewhere because of its use in the project. In case of severe unemployment that is expected to persist even when the develop-

2. Guidelines for estimating the accounting rate of interest are given in "Accounting Rate of Interest" in chapter ten. ☐

ment program is under way, the shadow wage would be zero and not whatever market wage is actually being paid. But such factors as seasonal fluctuations in demand for labor and varying degrees of labor mobility should caution against any hasty conclusion, even in such a case, that the opportunity cost of labor and the shadow wage rate are zero. Furthermore, the creation of one additional job in the urban sector may induce several workers in the rural sector to migrate to the town, so that the forgone output then becomes some multiple of one worker's marginal product. It is also likely that there will not be a single shadow wage rate in a country but rather a whole set of rates, for different skills and different times and locations.

The shadow wage rates thus measured may not represent the total cost to society of using labor on the project. Labor incomes may be higher as a consequence of the project, because project wages may exceed subsistence incomes or because projects may induce more productive self-employment. And an increase in labor incomes is likely to give rise to higher consumption and possibly some increase in savings. If, at the margin, consumption is considered less valuable than savings, this should be reflected in the shadow wage rate. In such a case an increase in consumption out of labor income is to some extent a cost that should be added to the shadow wage. The effect of this upward adjustment in the shadow wage rate will be to sacrifice some current employment and output in order to obtain faster growth—in line with the relevant value judgment.

There are other complications. If the project provides additional employment to the unemployed or to subsistence farmers, it is likely to give higher incomes to some of the poorest groups in society. If redress of poverty is considered important—and this, of course, is based again on a value judgment that the income distribution is not what it is desired to be, as well as a policy judgment that the distribution cannot be corrected effectively through fiscal means—this should be reflected by adjusting the shadow wage rate downward. Thus, the growth objective may require an upward adjustment, as argued in the previous paragraph, whereas the income distribution objective may require a downward adjustment in whatever level of the shadow wage rate would otherwise have been appropriate. This is not a contradiction but a straightforward reflection of the tradeoff between current output and employment and between growth and income distribution objectives.

Even in cases in which growth (savings) and income distribution considerations play no role, a shadow wage rate based on the marginal productivity of labor in alternative uses may be considered too simple. People may prefer unemployment to arduous work at low pay. This will depend on their income situation while unemployed, the value of leisure and leisure time activities such as fishing or fixing the roof, and the unpleasantness of the job. There is some "reservation wage" below which they will prefer being unemployed to taking the job. Should the government simply ignore this preference in its economic planning and decisionmaking? If not, the shadow wage rate may have to be higher than is indicated by a more narrow interpretation of opportunity cost of labor. Consequently, there will tend to be more voluntary unemployment than if society attached no value to leisure and to the possible disutility of at least certain kinds of work.

Traditional practice of the World Bank and other agencies in the shadow-pricing of labor has focused on the output of labor forgone in alternative uses. This practice implies a judgment that there is no significant reason for attaching a greater value, at the margin, to savings (growth) than to consumption; that the value attached to income distribution (or possibly to the expansion of employment in itself) does not require a reduction in the shadow wage rate below the marginal productivity of labor; and that preferences for work or for leisure can reasonably be ignored. (It might also reflect a judgment that any adjustments on these scores roughly cancel out.) In such cases it is good practice to make these judgments explicit. In many cases, however, it may be more appropriate to allow for these other factors in the determination of the shadow wage rate—and upward or downward adjustments should be made, as discussed earlier, in the rate established solely in relation to the marginal output of labor in alternative uses.[3] The basis for the adjustments and the judgments underlying them should always be indicated in the economic analysis of projects.[4]

FOREIGN AND DOMESTIC VALUES: TRADED AND NONTRADED GOODS

Some inputs of the project are directly imported or, though bought locally, lead to additional imports, since any domestic production of this input has reached capacity constraints. The cost of such goods to the economy (and therefore the shadow price) is the c.i.f.—cost insurance freight, representing the direct foreign exchange cost of the import—im-

3. The accounting rate of interest should then be adjusted to reflect the same judgments. □

4. The various elements of the shadow wage rate are discussed further in chapter eight, including the manner in which the derivation of the shadow wage rate depends on the assumptions that are considered appropriate in any particular case. Additional comments on estimating problems are given in chapter eleven. □

port price prevailing at the time the input is required. Similarly, the value to the economy of any output from the project that substitutes for imports is measured by the c.i.f. import price. Conversely, output that is directly exported or, though physically sold in the home market, leads to additional exports because domestic demand is fully met from existing supplies, has a value to the economy measured by the f.o.b.—free on board, the direct foreign exchange earnings of an export—export price. And, similarly again, for any input used in the project that would otherwise have been exported, the cost to the economy is the f.o.b. price.[5] In all such cases the c.i.f. or f.o.b. prices—that is, the border prices—should not be adjusted for any import duties or export taxes that may be levied: the import supply and export demand prices are the appropriate prices for project analysis. But these border prices should be adjusted, of course, to reflect internal transport or other costs in order to arrive at the value of the commodities at their point of origin (for outputs) and of destination (for inputs).

This summary assumes that the supply of imports or demand for exports is perfectly elastic, so that the project does not affect import or export prices. If import prices rise, however, or if export prices fall on account of the project, the value to the economy of additional imports or exports is not measured by the old or the new border price but is better approximated by the marginal import cost or export revenue.[6]

As a first approximation, any output or input whose value to the economy cannot be measured in terms of f.o.b. or c.i.f border prices should be assessed in relation to its price in the home market. This applies to obviously nontraded commodities such as electricity or transport, as well as to all commodities, usually those with high transport costs, whose domestic supply price, at the given level of local demand, is below the c.i.f. price of imports but above the f.o.b. price of exports. It also applies in cases in which government policy isolates commodities from foreign markets through import or export prohibitions or quotas. This price in the home market depends on local conditions of supply and demand, including market imperfections: monopolistic pricing, for example, affects power rates, as do import quotas on fuel imports and, less directly, general trade policies through their impact on such factor prices as wages.

As a result of market imperfections or indirect taxes, the marginal value (demand price) of nontraded inputs or outputs may differ from

5. In accordance with the chosen numéraire, as discussed in "Shadow Rate of Interest," above, such prices should be expressed in terms of the domestic currency equivalent (at the official rate of exchange). □
6. See "Tradables Subject to Finite Elasticities" in chapter nine. □

their marginal cost (supply price). The shadow price of such goods may be the demand price, the supply price, or somewhere in between—depending on whether project inputs or outputs affect the supply to other users, the supply from other producers, or both. If an input used in the project reduces the supply to other users, its shadow price should be based on the demand price; if the input is supplied from new production, its shadow price should be based on the supply price. With respect to both inputs and outputs, if the input is supplied from both sources, affecting other uses as well as calling forth new output, the shadow price is a weighted average of the demand price and supply price, the weights being determined by the elasticities of supply and demand.[7]

The shadow price of an output is determined similarly in relation to its demand or supply price, depending on whether additional output increases supply, reduces output from other producers, or both. With respect to both inputs and outputs, if at the margin supply is perfectly elastic or demand perfectly inelastic, the supply price is the shadow price. If at the margin supply is perfectly inelastic or demand perfectly elastic, the demand price should be used.[8]

In some cases indirect taxes (or subsidies) are designed to compensate for external costs (or benefits). If the tax (subsidy) corresponds exactly to the external cost (benefit) of an input, the shadow price of the input should include the tax (subsidy). Conversely, the shadow price of an output should in that case exclude the tax (subsidy). In other words, the cost of an input should be increased and the value of an output reduced by the amount of the external cost (tax). Similarly, subsidies that reflect external benefits should reduce the cost of inputs and increase the value of outputs. The taxes or subsidies, however, may provide only partial compensation or create other distortions. Therefore, it may often be preferable to treat such compensating taxes or subsidies as market distortions and allow separately for any externalities.

CONVERSION FACTORS AND SHADOW EXCHANGE RATES

Thus, with the qualifications noted above, the value to the economy of traded goods is measured by border prices, in local currency; that of nontraded goods is measured by domestic prices, in local currency. The final step is to convert border prices into domestic prices or vice versa.

What is the rationale for this conversion? Consider, for example, that

7. See "Accounting Prices for Nontraded Commodities," "Estimation of Marginal Social Cost," and "Estimation of Marginal Social Benefit" in chapter nine. □
8. This corresponds to the border price discussion for traded goods, above. □

a project increases demand for a nontraded commodity that is met in part by expanding its output and in part by a shift in consumption away from other uses. With respect to expanding output, the marginal social cost of increased production should be assessed. This is accomplished by valuing the inputs required to expand production at shadow prices. Traded inputs can be valued directly at border prices. Nontraded inputs can be further decomposed into their constituent inputs—unless they are drawn away from use elsewhere, in which case they must be treated in the manner described below—until all inputs consist of directly and indirectly traded goods and of basic domestic inputs (that is, mainly labor and possibly some other primary resources such as land, which are evaluated at their appropriate shadow prices).

With respect to the second part, a shift away from other uses, the forgone marginal social benefit of reduced consumption elsewhere should be assessed. This is accomplished by assessing the net social cost of the changes in producer and consumer surplus and related changes in expenditure patterns induced by the increase in price required to divert the nontraded input to the project.

The upshot of this whole procedure is that, in principle, the cost of the nontraded commodity used in the project can be expressed as the sum of the marginal social cost of increased production and the forgone marginal social benefit of reduced consumption induced by the increased demand of the project for the nontraded input.[9] In other words, the ratio between the cost of the nontraded good so estimated and its domestic price is the conversion factor for translating the domestic price of the nontraded good into its border-price equivalent.

Because an increase in demand for nontraded items will result in a social marginal cost of increased output and a forgone social marginal benefit of reduced consumption that will differ between nontraded goods depending on the input mix and the income effects involved, each nontraded good has, in principle, its own conversion factor.[10] There is, in principle, not one general conversion factor for all nontraded goods but a large set of such factors.

In practice, it is not feasible to differentiate conversion factors between all nontraded commodities. Shortcuts are needed that provide a reasonable approximation. In essence, all the shortcuts involve some degree of averaging for a group of nontraded items and, therefore, some degree of

9. A similar line of reasoning applies if the project increases the supply of the nontraded good instead of its demand, as in this example. □

10. Once again, a similar line of reasoning applies if the project increases the supply of the nontraded good. □

error if the average conversion factor is applied to a particular nontraded good rather than its own specific factor. For example, separate conversion factors might be estimated for broad groups of items such as construction, transportation, or consumption, possibly differentiated in consumption by the rich and by the poor. These approaches imply some differentiation in conversion factors applied to various nontraded goods. A more traditional approach ignores the need for differential conversion factors altogether and simply applies one conversion factor to all nontraded items. Since the chosen numéraire is in border prices rather than domestic prices, this conversion factor is the official exchange rate divided by the shadow exchange rate.[11]

The method for arriving at the standard conversion factor is already suggested by the foregoing discussion. It should represent some average or typical value of the conversion factors of individual nontraded goods. Since these factors reflect—leaving income effects aside—the ratios between the domestic and border prices of traded goods entering into the determination of the social value of the nontraded good, this value depends on the trade policies being pursued by the government.[12] For example, in the case of wide-ranging import restrictions, the official exchange rate understates the value to the economy of additional foreign exchange earnings. In other words, the shadow exchange rate of local currency per unit of foreign currency is then higher than the official rate. This is not a question of equilibrium: the official exchange rate is an equilibrium rate given the trade restrictions, but the shadow rate is higher. Export incentives have similar effects: widespread export subsidies tend to give a shadow exchange rate higher than the official rate.[13] If trade policies are anticipated to change over time, this should be reflected in corresponding changes in the shadow exchange rates. In the event of general trade liberalization, the shadow and official exchange rates would tend to merge—not at the existing official level, but at a new equilibrium level.

Estimates of the shadow exchange rate and hence the standard conversion factor are based on weighted averages of import tariffs and export subsidies, the weights being given by the relative importance of traded goods in nontraded production and consumption. As an approximation, weights may be based on the shares of imports and exports in

11. The corresponding traditional practice converts foreign exchange at the shadow exchange rate. □

12. Note also that normally tradable items may become nontraded if subject to rigid and binding quotas. □

13. Export taxes and import subsidies have the opposite effect. □

total trade. Traditional analytical practice of the World Bank and other agencies has normally used the general shadow exchange rate approach. Use of specific conversion factors is to be encouraged in cases in which greater accuracy of conversion is required.[14]

RENTS, PROFITS, AND OTHER CAPITAL INCOMES

In some cases the increase in demand for inputs in the project can be met by expanding output from plants working below capacity. The valuation of such inputs raises no new problems. They are valued as non-traded commodities, since their supply is not met by increasing imports or reducing exports. The cost of the inputs is determined by current operating costs, with each of its elements—say, fuel and labor—appropriately shadow priced: or, in other words, the relevant cost of the inputs is their short-run marignal social cost. There are no capital costs: the investment in the plant may be considered a sunk cost as long as the excess capacity continues. When capacity constraints begin to impose themselves or new investments become necessary to expand output, incremental operating costs alone are no longer an appropriate measure of the value of the inputs to the economy. At that point the scarcity value or rents earned on the inputs or the cost of additional investment should be included as costs.

Factors in fixed supply, such as land, mineral resources, or sites, may earn rents reflecting their scarcity value. To shadow-price primary factors in fixed supply, an estimate must be made of the opportunity cost to the economy of using these factors to satisfy project demand. The rent earned by these factors may or may not be an adequate measure of the appropriate shadow price; distortions in the product and capital markets may have to be taken into account to derive the shadow rental from the market rental. Similar considerations apply to other assets, such as roads or power plants, that are temporarily in fixed supply: costs are sunk, but strong demand may give the assets a high rent value. The shadow prices of their output—say, road services or power—cannot then be based on their operating costs only, but should include the scarcity value of the assets.

The shadow wage rate depends not only on direct opportunity cost relative to output forgone but also on other factors such as the impact

---

14. Guidelines for deriving and estimating the appropriate shadow exchange rate or conversion factors in the light of current and anticipated trade policies and other considerations are given in parts II and III. □

of additional employment on savings and income distribution.[15] The shadow value of rents, interest, and profits may have to be adjusted in a similar manner. This depends on who the recipients of such payments are, the amount of additional taxes due, the extent to which they save their after-tax incomes, whether such savings are considered more valuable than consumption, and the value attached to income accruing to them as compared with income accruing to others. Traditional analytical practice has not systematically incorporated these factors in its economic analysis of projects—except, to some extent, with respect to income accruing to foreigners. The implications of this approach and the underlying judgments on which it is based should always be made clear. Where income distribution and savings effects are considered relevant, they should be taken into account explicitly in the economic analysis.[16]

CONSUMER SURPLUS

The project may lower the price to consumers, in which case the shadow price corresponding to the new level of output is not a complete measure of the benefits to the economy, since it neglects the effect of the reduction in prices. Consumers would have been willing to pay more for the quantity of the product they now buy. Consumer surplus is a measure of the difference between what a consumer is prepared to pay for a product and what he actually pays. If the project lowers the price to consumers, they gain an increase in consumer surplus. This increase should be included as part of the benefits of the project.

Consumer surplus, however, is a private measure of the benefit derived from a reduction in price and does not necessarily correspond to its social value. If the government accords the same value to benefits regardless of the recipient of those benefits, the social and private measures will coincide; but, as has been shown in connection with the discussion on wages and capital incomes, the government may wish to assign a higher value to benefits accruing to poor people than to those accruing to rich people or a higher value to those benefits which will be translated into savings than to those which will be consumed.

Three important points should be stressed here. First, the revaluation of consumer surplus should be consistent with the assumptions relating to income distribution and growth that were incorporated in the estimate of shadow wage rates and capital incomes. Second, care should be taken

15. See "Shadow Wage Rates," above. □
16. Shadow rates for rents, interest, and profit payments are discussed further in part II. □

to identify the real beneficiaries of the consumer surplus on intermediate goods: a gain in consumer surplus by road users, for example, may in fact be an increase in their profits or in the profits of middlemen or shippers or an increase in surplus for consumers of the transported goods. Third, gains in consumer surplus, like other increases in income, lead to shifts in consumption expenditures. In principle, account should be taken of the costs (benefits) of increases (decreases) in consumption of other goods valued at their shadow costs.[17] In practice, correction by a standard conversion factor may be sufficient.

INFLATION

From the foregoing discussion of shadow prices it follows that the economic analysis of projects should not be based simply on present prices, but on the prices pertaining to each period. Thus, the analyst must project changes in shadow prices, taking into account the various considerations discussed previously. This should not be misunderstood: general changes in the price level that leave relative prices unchanged should not be taken into account. General inflation is not relevant for the economic analysis of projects insofar as it does not alter relative prices. But projected changes in relative (shadow) prices reflecting changes in the relation between supply and demand, whether or not associated with inflation, should enter into the economic analysis, since changes of this character indicate real shifts in the value of inputs and outputs to the economy. One apparent exception should be noted: any divergence between domestic and foreign inflation gives rise to a change in relative prices of traded goods (that is, border prices) and nontraded goods (that is, domestic prices). This, however, is a real change in relative prices only to the extent that differential rates of inflation are not offset by an adjustment in the exchange rate. □

---

17. In extreme cases, the social value of the consumer surplus could be more than offset by an increased cost of consumption. □

CHAPTER FOUR

Comparing Costs and Benefits: Investment Criteria

THOSE COSTS AND THOSE BENEFITS which should be included in the economic analysis of projects and how they should be valued or shadow-priced, have been discussed in the foregoing chapters. This discussion provides a basis for estimating time streams of costs and benefits, appropriately shadow-priced to reflect their value to the economy, given the government's basic objectives and the resources at its disposal. Among the basic questions of cost-benefit analysis there is left for consideration only how these costs and benefits streams are to be compared and what criteria are to be used in deciding whether a project represents a good use of resources.

NET PRESENT VALUE AND ECONOMIC RATE OF RETURN

The basic technique is to discount costs and benefits occurring in different periods and express them all in a common value at any one point of time. The relevant discount rate for this purpose has been discussed above.[1] If the net present value of the project is negative—that is, if the discounted value of the benefits is less than the discounted value of the costs—the project should be rejected. But in practice, projects with a positive (or zero) net present value should not necessarily be accepted, for two reasons.

First, the shadow prices of some inputs, such as land or site value or mineral resources, are virtually impossible to estimate independent of the project appraisal process itself. Consequently, the opportunity cost of such inputs may be seriously underestimated because their best alternative use may not have been identified. In principle, the relevant alternative use should be determined by a careful analysis of all conceivable projects; in practice, however, only a few alternatives can be examined. Nevertheless, it should be borne in mind that a high net present value may reflect an inadequate search for alternative projects rather than a potentially valuable project.

1. See "Shadow Rate of Interest" in chapter three. □

Second, there are many projects that by their nature are mutually exclusive: if one is chosen, the other cannot be undertaken. This applies to different designs or sizes or timings of what is essentially the same project. It also applies, perhaps less obviously, to such cases as plants in alternative locations serving the same limited market, surface irrigation development ruling out tubewell irrigation, and river development upstream instead of downstream. In all cases of mutually exclusive projects it is not sufficient to chose a project with a positive net present value; rather, the project with the highest net present value among the mutually exclusive alternatives should be selected. The analyst should not assume too easily that such mutually exclusive alternatives do not exist.

This discussion bears on the issue of ranking of projects in order of priority. This is a rather ambiguous notion. For a given investment budget and associated shadow prices, including the shadow rate of interest, projects either are acceptable in accordance with the foregoing criteria and should be included in the investment program or are not acceptable and should be excluded. This applies to mutually exclusive projects where only the project with the greatest net present value qualifies, as well as to any other projects that require only a nonnegative net present value. The only ranking in such instances is between the "ins" and the "outs."

A more interesting issue of ranking involves determination of which projects should successively be excluded (or included) if the investment budget were reduced (or expanded). A change in the size of the available investment budget implies, however, a change in the shadow rate of interest and corresponding changes in other shadow prices, which affects the size of the net present value of various projects in a differential way, depending on their time pattern and composition of inputs and outputs. Consequently, some projects with a high net present value in the original set of accepted projects (or program) may now drop out, some projects with more moderate net present value may be retained, and some projects that previously were excluded may now qualify. There is no single ranking of projects that are added or deleted from the program in accordance with variations in its size. Changes in the investment budget tend to affect its general composition and not simply marginal projects.

Traditional analytical practice has calculated the economic rate of return: that is, the rate of discount that results in a zero net present value for the project.[2] If this rate of return exceeds the estimated shadow rate of interest, it indicates for a nonmutually exclusive project that it is ac-

_____

2. This rate is usually referred to in the literature as the internal (economic) rate of return. □

ceptable; the net present value is then positive. Unfortunately, the rate of return is defective as a measure of the relative merits of mutually exclusive projects; a higher rate of return does not necessarily indicate the superior alternative as measured by the size of the surplus when costs and benefits are discounted at the shadow rate of interest. The economic rate of return thus may be misleading in comparing the economic merits of alternative projects and should not be used for this most essential function of project analysis.[3] The (internal) economic rate of return, however, is a widely understood concept and has merit as a compact summary measure of the economic result of a project. For this purpose alone, its use should be continued.

Both measures—the net present value and the economic rate of return—are sometimes misinterpreted. The essential purpose of project analysis is to sort out the best of the feasible alternatives: that is, the project that makes the greatest contribution to the basic objectives of the country's economy. After the selection has been made on this basis, this contribution may be expressed as a net present value or economic rate of return by comparing it with the situation without the project; this will give some indication of the increase in rent (surplus) earned by the primary factors as compared with what they would otherwise have earned.

But it should be noted that, first, the net present value or rate of return does not necessarily measure the contribution of the project in comparison with that of other (rejected) alternatives that may in fact have surpluses over the without situation nearly as large as the selected project; second, the definition of what would have happened without the project is not altogether unambiguous; and, third, the size of the surplus or net present value may be greatly affected by the estimated cost of such primary factors as land or mineral resources, which would often reflect costs of opportunities forgone in alternative uses other than that of the without situation alone.

COST MINIMIZATION

Special variants of mutually exclusive projects are alternatives that produce the same benefits. They may involve a question of choice of de-

---

3. Benefit-cost ratios are similarly misleading, and they suffer as well from other ambiguities; thus, they should not be used. This also applies to traditional business criteria (such as the payback period) that are wrong indicators of economic profitability. The economic rate of return criterion can provide the correct decisions if applied to the difference in net benefits between two mutually exclusive projects. But in such cases the possibility of multiple solutions to the rate of return calculation is considerably increased. □

sign, such as between hydro or thermal power generation, rail or road transport: whichever technical solution is chosen, the benefits are deemed to be the same. In such cases it is necessary only to consider costs and select the alternative with the lowest present value of cost when discounted at the appropriate rate of interest. For any given level of output and benefits, the least-cost alternative is to be preferred. But by itself this tells nothing about the economic merits of the project: even the least-cost project may have costs that exceed its benefits. The analysis should therefore not stop at a least-cost solution but wherever possible consider whether benefits are adequate. In cases in which valuation of the benefits is difficult—for example, improvements in health services— an assessment of the (least) cost per unit of physical output (such as number of beds made available or reduction in morbidity) may be helpful.[4] But note that differences in costs as between the least-cost design and the next best alternative are not, and should not be used as a substitute for, a proper measure of the benefits of such projects.

FIRST-YEAR RETURN

An important choice of project alternatives concerns timing: when should the project be undertaken? In principle, alternative starting dates for the project, as well as other variations in execution such as stage construction, are subject to the normal net present value test—with all net present values being calculated for the same base year, irrespective of the different starting dates of the projects.

In some instances, however, a simpler test may suffice to determine the appropriate timing of the project. The first-year return test involves calculating the ratio of net first-year benefits to investment costs. If the ratio is below (or above) the appropriate rate of interest, the project is premature (or overdue). The test is strictly accurate only if benefits are time dependent (and rising) rather than project dependent and project costs are not affected by postponement. In other words, the benefit stream must not shift depending on when the project is undertaken, and "tail-end effects" resulting from the timing of the project must be negligible. If these conditions are not fulfilled, the first-year return test is not applicable.

This test, of course, is not a substitute for the standard requirement

---

4. The analyst might also compute the value that would have to be attached to, say, the benefits from hospital beds in order to make the net present value zero. □

that the project have a positive net present value; it is only a complementary test to determine its optimal timing.

EQUIVALENT CRITERIA

As discussed earlier, the net present value and the economic rate of return are two different ways of presenting the same information. The first is a measure of the project's value when due allowance has been made for all costs; the second is a measure of the project's value when due allowance has been made for all costs except the interest cost on capital. It follows that the critical point for acceptance or rejection of a project on the first scale is zero,[5] whereas it is the accounting rate of interest on the second scale.

Tests similar to that of economic rate of return could be derived for factors of production other than capital. For example, net benefits can be related to labor inputs (or foreign exchange inputs) by netting out all costs and benefits other than labor (or foreign exchange). The critical point for acceptance or rejection then becomes the shadow wage rate (or shadow exchange rate). All such tests are equivalent as long as the valuations of inputs and outputs remain the same and provide no new information; they are simply transformations of the original net present value test. Hence, information on the employment or foreign exchange effects of a project should not be presented as a contribution, beneficial or otherwise, to the country's development objectives in addition to that contribution measured by the net present value or the economic rate of return. The weight attached to employment or foreign exchange earnings is already fully reflected in the shadow prices used in the calculation of net present value.

Similarly, the effect of the project on investment and consumption is already adequately captured through the use of shadow prices. If the government values savings more highly than consumption, this is reflected in the shadow wage rate and valuation of profits and in the accounting rate of interest. Therefore, it is fully taken into account in the calculation of the project's net present value. Discussion of the project's effects on saving and consumption must be consistent with the assumptions and data used in the calculation of net present value. Consumption effects are, of course, closely related to employment effects. □

5. This disregards the qualifications discussed early in this chapter: that in practice the rent elements of cost are not normally included. □

CHAPTER FIVE

Uncertainty, Sensitivity, and Risk

UNCERTAINTY IS INHERENT in project analysis. Estimates of costs and demand, of shadow prices and the parameters underlying them, and of consumer surplus and externalities are approximate even for the present, and uncertainty increases when those estimates are projected into the future, as the analysis requires. A question, therefore, is how this uncertainty is to be taken into account in the choice of projects.

As a starting point, the basic calculation of the net present value should incorporate the best estimates of the variables and parameters that determine the cost and benefit streams. The estimates should be the expected value obtained, in principle, by weighting each possible value by the probability of its occurrence.[1] This ensures that the estimates are unbiased. Biased estimates—such as conservative estimates of costs (that is, on the high side) and of benefits (on the low side)—should be avoided as much as possible, since they distort the comparison of alternative projects.

Actual values may deviate from the best estimates: that is, from the expected values. It is important to investigate the impact of such deviations on the net present value of the project. A simple method is to vary the magnitude of the more important variables, singly or in combinations, by a certain percentage and then to determine how sensitive the net present value is to such changes; or alternatively, to determine by how much a variable must change for the net present value to be reduced to zero. Such sensitivity analysis helps to provide a better understanding of the critical elements on which the outcome of the project depends. It may focus attention on the variables for which a further effort should be made to firm up the estimates and narrow down the range of uncertainty. It also may aid the management of the project by indicating critical areas that require close supervision to ensure the expected favorable return to the economy. The number of variables to be tested in this fashion is a matter of judgment, but care should be taken that all the plausible cases are covered. In particular, the significance of a certain sensitivity—

---

1. The expected value is not the same, in general, as the "most likely" value, in the sense of the mode of the distribution. □

that is, the change in net present value resulting from, say, a 10 percent change in a certain variable—depends not only on its magnitude but also on the range of values that the variable is considered likely to attain; and some variables are likely to move together or in opposite directions in response to a common cause or because of close interrelations.

These interrelations point to the weakness of sensitivity analysis that shows the effect on the net present value of a project if certain variables were to assume different values, all other things remaining equal. It does not show the combined net effect of changes in all variables or the likelihood of various changes occurring together. Risk analysis, or probability analysis, is designed to throw light on these questions. It requires specifying, as well as possible, probabilities for the several values that may be attained by each variable entering into the project analysis, as well as any covariances between the variables: that is, the extent to which changes in one variable are correlated with changes in the other. (Specifying these covariances tends to be a stumbling block in practice.) Given these probability distributions, specific values of the underlying variables are randomly selected and combined into an estimate of the net present value of a project. Repeated application of this process produces a probability distribution of the net present value (or rate of return): that is, the probability that the net present value will take on certain values higher or lower than the central expected value calculated in the basic analysis. This process gives the decisionmaker a better picture of the degree of risk involved in the project than is given by a single valued calculation. It enables judgments that there is an X percent chance that the project will result in a negative net present value and a Y percent chance of a surplus exceeding $N million.

Risk analysis provides a better basis for judging the relative merits of alternative projects—but it does nothing to diminish the risks. Some risks, of course, can be reduced by further investigations—of, for example, the technical problems and costs or the market prospects. This may or may not be worthwhile, depending on the cost of the investigation and the expected reduction in risk and the value attached thereto. Risk may also be reduced by a flexible design of the project that leaves future options open so that unexpected changes in circumstances can be coped with better. Such flexible design is likely to impose additional costs that—in view of the anticipated uncertainties and the benefits of greater responsiveness that the flexible design makes possible—may or may not be justified.

In traditional analytical practice, sensitivity analysis is a standard part of project analysis, as a check on the results of a project if crucial variables were to differ from the estimated expected values used in the analysis. More elaborate risk analysis is undertaken only in special cases. It should be considered for larger more complex projects or projects having exceptional risks that cannot be adequately appreciated by means of a simple sensitivity analysis. The advantages of further study of certain project features or variables and of a more flexible design to cope better with future uncertainties should be part of the normal process of project preparation and appraisal.

Finally, the use of net present expected value as a measure of a project's worth implies that the government is indifferent to risk as measured by, say, the variance of expected value. This is justifiable provided the risks of all public sector projects are pooled and spread over the country's entire population so that a change in the outcome of any single project is unlikely to have a significant impact on the income of any single group. This, however, is not necessarily true for all projects. In some cases—agricultural projects, for example—the risk may be borne by a relatively small section of the population; in other cases, the success or failure of the project may weigh heavily on national income. In such cases, it may be desirable to assess the cost of offsetting risk by, for example, maintaining sufficient foreign exchange reserves to offset fluctuations in export prices.   □

PART II

Derivation of Shadow Prices

THIS PART PROVIDES a self-contained explanation of shadow-pricing. It is intended to give the person involved in the economic analysis of projects an intuitive appreciation of the techniques being recommended, but it should not be viewed as a rigorous statement of the subject, nor should it be assumed that all eventualities are covered. More detailed information on the technical derivation of shadow prices is provided in the appendix, in which some of the complications omitted from this section are also considered. Possible methods of estimation are described in part III. The definition of symbols used throughout the remainder of the book is presented in the glossary of symbols on page 149.

CHAPTER SIX

Integration of Efficiency and Equity in Project Selection

TRADITIONAL ANALYTICAL PRACTICE has focused on efficiency or income maximization as the sole criterion of merit in the selection of projects. More recently, however, the distribution of benefits among different income groups has become a serious issue in the eyes of both politicians and economists. This increasing concern with equity raises at least two questions with regard to project selection. First, under what conditions can project selection be conducted without reference to the distribution of project benefits? (That is, under what conditions is the traditional analytical approach appropriate?) Second, if project selection must take account of the distribution of project benefits, what is the most appropriate way of including considerations of equity in project selection and yet at the same time giving due allowance to considerations of efficiency? These questions are addressed in this chapter.

DEFINITION OF SHADOW PRICES

Shadow prices are defined as the increase in welfare resulting from any marginal change in the availability of commodities or factors of production. Thus, the process of shadow-pricing presupposes, first, a well-defined social welfare function, expressed as a mathematical statement of the country's objectives, so that the marginal changes can be evaluated; and, second, a precise understanding of the constraints and policies that determine the country's development, both now and in the future, and hence the existing or projected circumstances in which the marginal changes will occur. The particular type of welfare function and those constraints which are generally regarded as the most important in the less developed countries are discussed below.

SOCIAL WELFARE FUNCTIONS

Governments make decisions every day related to some conception of welfare. Usually the conception of welfare is not clearly defined; as a result, decisions are often contradictory. A clear statement of the welfare function therefore is essential to ensure consistent decisionmaking. Countries have many objectives, such as better health services and more efficient agriculture, but such objectives are really means to attain more fundamental objectives that usually relate to the distribution of consumption both over time and at a point of time. It is these two aspects of consumption—that is, its intertemporal and interpersonal distribution—which form the basis of the welfare function employed here. This permits concentration on the crucial tradeoff between growth (that is, the transformation of present consumption into future consumption) and the redistribution of present consumption (that is, the transfer of consumption from the rich to the poor).

CONSTRAINTS

Constraints can take various forms. All economies are confronted by basic constraints on the availability of resources and the possibilities for their technological transformation. In some circumstances market prices will correctly reflect the scarcity value of these resources, but other constraints often operate to divorce market prices and economic values. Minimum wage legislation, for example, may keep the market wage above the forgone output in other occupations. Similarly, trade taxes cause a divergence between the value of commodities at domestic and international prices, as a result of which the official exchange rate does not adequately reflect the value of foreign exchange.

To correct for such distortions the economist recommends the use of shadow prices: that is, of prices that will ensure the efficient allocation of resources despite the distortion. But shadow prices as defined here do not necessarily assume the removal of the distortion. The attempt is not to estimate, for example, the free trade exchange rate (unless the country is expected to adopt a free-trade policy) but rather an exchange rate that—given the distortion—will more accurately reflect the value of foreign exchange.

Less developed countries may be constrained in other ways as well. Administrative costs or political pressure, for example, may limit the government's actions. Thus, the possibilities of taxing the agricultural sector may be limited by the costs of collection and administration, or the political power of the rich may be sufficient to prevent the government from redistributing income to the poor. Arguments of this type suggest that less developed countries may also be faced by a fiscal constraint in the sense that the government cannot raise sufficient revenue to achieve its desired level of investment or its desired redistribution of income. The obvious implication is that the government may wish to use project selection as an alternative, additional method of increasing public income or of redistributing income. Even within the public sector, constraints may prevent the optimal use of the limited public revenue. The government may be committed to various expenditures (for example, payment of civil servants' salaries) so that public sector expenditure in other directions (for example, investment) may be constrained below its optimal level.

If such constraints are thought to be important, the value of a project depends not only on the benefits generated by the project but also on their distribution. In other words, the effect on the incomes of different groups in society (that is, the distribution effect) must be looked at as well as the effect of the project on the allocation of resources (that is, the efficiency effect). Until recently the World Bank and other agencies concerned with project analysis have been interested primarily in the efficiency aspect of projects, but it is now recommended that project analysts also examine the distributional implications of projects. Project analysts ought now to calculate the project's net present social profit, where the adjective "social" indicates that considerations of both efficiency and distribution have been taken into account in arriving at a measure of the project's worth.

GENERAL RATIONALE OF DISTRIBUTION WEIGHTS

The following paragraphs contain an outline of the general rationale for the inclusion of income distribution weights in project selection and broadly describe the manner in which this aspect of the analysis can be introduced into the standard appraisal methods. The detailed derivation of distribution weights is deferred to the following chapter.

The proposed use of distribution weights in project appraisal raises the question of the circumstances in which such weights are necessary. If, for example, the government values all income equally regardless of its distribution—either between the public and private sector or within the private sector—the need for distribution weights disappears. The weights themselves, however, only apparently disappear; in reality they are still there, but the implicit value judgments made are such that the social cost of each resource transfer is exactly offset by the resulting social benefit.

Many people would consider it rather extreme not to assign different values to marginal increments in consumption accruing to different income groups. Another point of view, however, argues for excluding distribution weights. If the government, through its control of fiscal policy, is able to redistribute income costlessly, no need exists to include distribution weights in project selection; project selection should under such circumstances aim to maximize income and allow the fiscal system to redistribute it in a desirable fashion.

It is argued here, however, that, in general, redistribution can never be costless and that, in particular, redistribution in developing countries may be so costly as to be prohibitive. With regard to the general argument, all fiscal measures have an administrative cost and, at least in principle, a cost resulting from an unfavorable effect on incentives. With regard to the particular argument, the very unequal distribution of income-consumption in most developing countries and the difficulty of raising additional revenue indicate severe constraints on the government's use of the fiscal system. These constraints typically reflect an inability to raise sufficient revenue because to do so is not administratively feasible and an inability to tax the rich sufficiently because of that group's political power. Moreover, the general fiscal system of most developing countries (and, in fact, most developed countries) cannot possibly reallocate the benefits and costs of projects as varied and geographically dispersed as those usually found in these countries. If these arguments are accepted (rejected), distribution weights are (are not) required for project selection.

When distribution weights are considered necessary, they may be introduced into the standard economic analysis of projects in the following fashion. Assume that a project lasts one year and results in a net increase of E in real resources available to the economy. If interest lies only in efficiency, the increase in real resources is an adequate measure of project benefits. But if there is interest in income distribution as well, the distribution of resources among different groups in society must also be examined. The resources accruing to each group can then be weighted in accordance with the appropriate concept of social welfare and summed to obtain the measure of the project's social worth.

To determine the distribution of real resources, the distribution of financial net benefits must be examined, because this will determine who has control over the increase in real resources. Obviously, the financial benefits will accrue either to the public sector or to the private sector, and, within the private sector, they will accrue either to the rich or to the poor. Assume, for example, that as a result of the project the income of one particular group in the private sector is increased by C and that all other net financial benefits accrue to the public sector.[1] Assume further that the private sector allocates the entire increase in income to con-

---

1. For a definition of symbols, see the glossary of symbols. □

sumption.[2] The increased consumption will comprise various commodities or services that will have a cost in real resources, which may or may not equal C. Given the many distortions in the product and factor markets of less developed countries, it may be necessary to adjust C, the financial measure of the increase in consumption, to obtain its real resource cost. Let the adjustment factor be β, so that the private sector enjoys an increase in real resources of $C\beta$, and the public sector retains control over the remainder: that is, $E - C\beta$.

To measure the social value of these changes reference must be made to the social welfare function. Assume that the increase in social welfare resulting from a marginal increase in the availability of real resources to the public sector is W_g, and that the social welfare resulting from a marginal increase in the availability of consumption to the particular income group is W_c. The measure of social benefits is then: $(E - C\beta)W_g + CW_c$. Although W_g is defined for real resources, W_c is defined for consumption at market prices. This simply reflects the fact that the public sector is concerned primarily with increases in real resources, whereas the private sector derives its utility from consumption possibilities as determined by market prices.[3]

NUMÉRAIRE

Social benefits then should be expressed in a common yardstick, or numéraire. Any commodity or resource may be chosen as this unit of account, but, once it has been chosen, all values must consistently be expressed in that numéraire. It is recommended that as numéraire the value of real resources that are freely available to the public sector be used: that is, we want to set the weight assigned to $(E - C\beta)$ equal to unity. To do this and to maintain all price relativities, we divide throughout by W_g, so that the measure of social benefits (S) in the chosen numéraire is:

(1) $S = (E - C\beta) + C\omega,$

$$\begin{bmatrix} Net\ social \\ benefits \end{bmatrix} = \begin{bmatrix} Increase\ in\ real \\ resources\ in \\ public\ sector \end{bmatrix} + \begin{bmatrix} Social\ welfare \\ from\ increased \\ private\ sector\ consumption \end{bmatrix}$$

where W_c/W_g has been replaced by ω. Thus, a unit of private consump-

2. An increase in private savings is treated separately: that is, for the moment it is assumed that there is no saving out of private income. See "Value of Private Savings" in chapter seven. □

3. W_c, however, will express the social value of the increase in private welfare. □

tion expressed in domestic prices (for example, C) has to be revalued by, in this case, ω to express it in the numéraire. This may appear tedious, but, if consumption expressed in domestic prices were used as numéraire, the reverse process would have to be gone through in order to express $(E-C\beta)$ in the consumption numéraire.[4]

EFFICIENCY AND SOCIAL PRICES

For practical purposes, it is more convenient to rewrite equation (1) in the following manner:

(2) $S=E-C\,(\beta-\omega).$

$$\begin{bmatrix} Net\ social \\ benefits \end{bmatrix} = \begin{bmatrix} Net\ efficiency \\ benefits \end{bmatrix} - \begin{bmatrix} Net\ social\ cost \\ of\ increased\ private \\ sector\ consumption \end{bmatrix}$$

This has the advantage of separately identifying the efficiency benefits, E. Thus, the project economist-analyst can begin by estimating efficiency benefits as has been done in the past. The only other item he must estimate is the increase in net income accruing to the various income groups in the private sector who are affected by the project. The other elements of equation (2)—β and ω—will then either be provided by the national planning office or else be derived from a standard table.

Thus, the mechanics of this approach are fairly simple. Alternatively, but equivalently, the distributional element of projects can be included in the definition of shadow prices on the grounds that all financial benefits must accrue to the factors of production employed by the project. For example, assume that the increase in income, C, generated by the project actually accrues as a result of increased wage payments to labor. The efficiency cost of employing labor—that is, forgone marginal product of labor—is netted out in obtaining the net increase in resources, E. In addition, employing labor involves a net social cost of increased consumption. Thus, the social cost of the labor input can be defined as: social cost=efficiency cost+$C(\beta-\omega)$. And if the increase in consump-

---

4. If account is to be taken of the distribution of consumption, the numéraire would have to be defined as the value of consumption at a particular level of consumption. The public income numéraire is used in I. M. D. Little and J. A. Mirrlees, *Project Appraisal and Planning for the Developing Countries* (London: Heinemann Educational Books, 1974), the general format of which has been followed here. The consumption numéraire is used in United Nations Industrial Development Organization, *Guidelines for Project Evaluation* (New York: United Nations, 1972). For additional references to the literature, see the bibliography. □

tion per worker is c, then the social price per worker is: social price = efficiency price + $c(\beta - \omega)$.[5] This latter method may be useful for some factors such as unskilled labor, for which it is convenient to have an all-inclusive price for purposes of decentralized decisionmaking, and may be essential for at least one price, the discount rate. For other factors this may not be particularly interesting, in which case the first method could be used. Although both methods may be used in any single project, they must not be used for the same factor payment because this would involve double counting.

Although detailed discussion of the distribution weights is deferred until chapter seven, some general implications of the approach outlined above can be considered at this stage. First, if the increase in consumption, c, is zero, the social price equals the efficiency price.[6] This might occur in a perfect labor market in which the transfer of labor involves no change in income or consumption. Second, if the wage earner spends all his income on, say, duty-free imports or, more generally, in nondistorted markets, then β equals unity. In other words, β can be viewed as a factor that corrects for market distortions, especially those caused by trade tariffs. β may vary for different consumers depending on the actual composition of their consumption basket. Third, if the government is interested in income distribution, ω will tend to be low for the rich and high for the poor, and at some consumption level the situation $\omega = \beta$ would obtain, so that the real resource cost incurred by the government, $c\beta$, and the social benefit enjoyed by the worker, $c\omega$, as a result of a marginal increase in consumption are exactly offsetting. This level of consumption is known as the "critical consumption level": the social price equals the efficiency price at the critical consumption level. Fourth, as has been seen, the government may not wish to include distribution weights in project selection, in which case the social price always equals the efficiency price. (This has been the case in traditional analytical practice of the World Bank and other lending institutions.)

In presenting the economic analysis of a project, it will be instructive to indicate the project's worth at market, at efficiency, and at social prices. The first evaluation will correspond to the financial appraisal of the project. The second will be similar to that traditionally used by the Bank and other agencies: that is, all incomes will be considered equally

---

5. Efficiency price is used in the traditional sense of opportunity cost: that is, the forgone marginal product per worker. The terms "shadow" and "accounting" are used indiscriminately to refer to both efficiency and social price. □
6. Throughout this paragraph comments applying to social and efficiency prices also apply to social and efficiency benefits as defined by equation (2). □

valuable, there will be no premium on public income or investment, the discount rate will be the opportunity cost of capital, and other factor prices will be based on opportunity cost. In other words, the evaluation at efficiency prices corrects for the distortions in factor and product markets but does not assume any constraint on the government's ability to redistribute income or to invest. The third evaluation will include the project's distributional impact (see equation [2]) if it is thought that the economy does suffer from a fiscal constraint.

Inasmuch as the main innovation is contained in this final step, particular attention will be paid to the derivation of distribution weights, with chapter seven devoted entirely to a discussion of both interpersonal and intertemporal weights. This is not to say, of course, that the methodology ignores efficiency: to illustrate this, in chapter eight efficiency and distributional considerations are examined together for the shadow prices of labor. Finally, in chapter nine the prices to be used for commodities, both tradable and nontradable, are examined.   □

CHAPTER SEVEN

Derivation of Weights

THE INTEGRATION OF considerations of efficiency and equity in project selection having been examined at a general level, it is possible to focus on the detailed derivation of a complete system of distribution weights. This chapter demonstrates how both interpersonal and intertemporal distribution weights may be derived from an explicitly specified welfare function. The demonstration concludes with an example in which the derivation of a complete system of distribution weights for two economies is shown to reflect fully the different objectives and circumstances of those economies.

DEFINITION OF THE NUMÉRAIRE

The choice of numéraire—or unit of account—is basic to the determination of the weights, insofar as the numéraire determines the absolute level of the weights. We recommended earlier that the value of real resources available to the public sector be used as numéraire—or, put more simply, that the numéraire be public income. Not all public income, however, is equally valuable. For example, the public income generated by a particular project may be earmarked for a particular purpose and may therefore be less valuable than public income that is not so earmarked. Moreover, some public income may accrue in the form of domestic currency, which may not be as valuable as public income that accrues either in the form of foreign exchange or in a form that is freely convertible into foreign exchange at the official exchange rate.

More precisely, therefore, the numéraire is defined here as uncommitted public income measured in convertible currency, which will be referred to often as "free foreign exchange." It is merely a matter of convenience whether this convertible currency is expressed in units of the local or some foreign currency. Here all currency will be expressed in local currency at the official exchange rates. Thus, when "free foreign exchange" is mentioned, it should not be thought of (unless clearly so indicated) as so many dollars or yen but as their equivalent value in units of the domestic currency, at the official exchange rate.

One further aspect of the numéraire must be clarified. The numéraire, like any other yardstick, is useful only if its value remains constant over time. Hence, the numéraire, public income, must be so defined that it retains a constant purchasing power. This requires specification of the bundle of goods over which public income is to retain constant purchasing power in such a way that the price deflator index may be calculated by reference to the change in the value of this bundle of goods at accounting prices. We recommend, for practical reasons, that the price index be based on the bundle of goods and services bought at the margin of consumption expenditure.[1] If the value of this bundle, measured at accounting prices (and in units of local currency), rises because of inflation or devaluation, the current accounting values of costs and benefits should be deflated accordingly in order to express them in terms of the numéraire of constant purchasing power.[2]

Given the definition of the numéraire, an increased demand for, or supply of, commodities or services that affect only international trade can be immediately valued or costed relative to the quantity of foreign exchange that they produce or consume: that is, they can be immediately measured in terms of the numéraire. Other commodities or services, however, may have their main effects on domestic prices and hence domestic production and consumption rather than trade. Such items can also be expressed in foreign exchange, although the conversion is more complex (as will be seen later). In the earlier discussion of the social benefits of a project, the efficiency benefits, E, were implicitly expressed in foreign exchange, along the lines set out above. But the value of the increase in private consumption measured at domestic prices, C, must be converted into the numéraire by use of the net weight $(\beta - \omega)$, where β shows the cost and ω the welfare benefit of this increase in consumption as measured by the numéraire.[3] The conversion factor, β, is considered in the following section and the weight ω is discussed in detail in the six subsequent sections.

DERIVATION OF β

The value of β is determined by estimating the increase in the value of consumption at domestic prices if one more unit of foreign exchange

---

1. More precisely, since marginal consumption patterns vary between income levels, we recommend that the price index be based on the accounting value of marginal consumption at the critical consumption level. □
2. The estimation and use of appropriate price deflators is discussed further in part III. □
3. For a definition of symbols, see the glossary of symbols on page 149. □

is committed to consumption. Consumers may increase their consumption of exportables, importables, or nontradables. To the extent that different income groups will buy different bundles of goods at the margin of their expenditure, and given that trade distortions are different for different commodities, a different β should be estimated for different income groups. In practice, however, a separate β for rich and poor income groups will probably be sufficient.

Calculating β requires information on the (marginal) consumption pattern, the required number being the ratio of the value of this consumption at border prices to its value at domestic prices. Thus, if tradable commodities—that is, commodities that at the margin are being exported or imported—form part of consumption, the ratio will depend on the import-export tax or subsidy. But if nontradables appear in the consumption pattern, more complicated methods must be applied, such as valuing the inputs used in the production of nontradables at border prices.[4] To a reasonable approximation, especially if nontradable consumption is small, the following can be written:

$$(3) \quad \beta = \frac{M+X}{M(1+t_m)+X(1-t_x)},$$

$$\begin{bmatrix} Consumption \\ conversion \\ factor \end{bmatrix} = \begin{bmatrix} Value\ of\ imports \\ plus\ exports\ at \\ border\ prices \end{bmatrix} \div \begin{bmatrix} Value\ of\ imports \\ plus\ exports\ at \\ domestic\ prices \end{bmatrix}$$

where $M(X)$ is the c.i.f. value of imports (f.o.b. value of exports) in the marginal consumption bundle, and $t_m(t_x)$ is the average tax on imports (exports), which may be measured by the ratio of the revenue from trade and other taxes on consumption goods to the value of those consumption goods c.i.f. or f.o.b.[5] Although the use of equation (3) to estimate β is a convenient shortcut, it might also lead to misleading results. The analyst should ensure that the basket of commodities (and their respective tax rates) is a reasonable reflection of the consumption basket of the particular income class in question.[6]

4. Such complications are explained more fully in "Accounting Prices for Nontraded Commodities" in chapter nine. □

5. β translates domestic prices into border prices expressed in units of the domestic currency. Division by the official exchange rate is required to obtain foreign exchange proper. □

6. β and its relation to the shadow exchange rate are discussed further in "Standard Conversion Factor (SCF)" in chapter nine. □

MEANING OF ω

The purpose of ω is to indicate the value of a marginal increase in consumption of a particular group in the private sector measured at domestic prices relative to the numéraire: that is, relative to the value of free foreign exchange in the public sector. If the welfare value of the private sector group's consumption is W_c and that of public sector income is W_g,[7] the choice of numéraire implies that:

(4) $\omega = W_c / W_g.$

$$\begin{bmatrix} \textit{Value of private} \\ \textit{sector consumption} \\ \textit{at consumption} \\ \textit{level c relative} \\ \textit{to the numéraire} \end{bmatrix} = \begin{bmatrix} \textit{Marginal social} \\ \textit{value of private} \\ \textit{sector consumption} \\ \textit{at consumption} \\ \textit{level c} \end{bmatrix} \div \begin{bmatrix} \textit{Marginal social} \\ \textit{value of foreign} \\ \textit{exchange in} \\ \textit{the public} \\ \textit{sector} \end{bmatrix}$$

To evaluate this ratio, direct estimates of W_c and W_g could be attempted; however, it may be more convenient to adopt a slightly different approach. In particular, we will divide the derivation of ω into two steps. First, define v as the value of a marginal increase in public income measured in free foreign exchange (W_g) divided by the value of a marginal increase in consumption at domestic prices to someone at the average level of consumption ($W_{\bar{c}}$, where the bar indicates average); that is:

(5) $v = W_g / W_{\bar{c}}.$

$$\begin{bmatrix} \textit{Value of the} \\ \textit{numéraire relative} \\ \textit{to private sector} \\ \textit{consumption at} \\ \textit{the average level} \\ \textit{of consumption} \end{bmatrix} = \begin{bmatrix} \textit{Marginal social} \\ \textit{value of foreign} \\ \textit{exchange in} \\ \textit{the public} \\ \textit{sector} \end{bmatrix} \div \begin{bmatrix} \textit{Marginal social} \\ \textit{value of private} \\ \textit{sector consumption} \\ \textit{at the average} \\ \textit{level of consumption} \end{bmatrix}$$

Thus, a marginal increase in consumption at domestic prices to someone at the average level of consumption is worth $1/v$ units of the numéraire. Second, to obtain the value of a marginal increase in consumption at domestic prices to someone at some level of consumption other than the average level, define d as the value (W_c) of a marginal increase in consumption at domestic prices to someone at a level of consumption, c, divided by the value ($W_{\bar{c}}$) of a marginal increase in consumption at

---

7. Thus, W_g measures the increase in aggregate welfare resulting from a marginal increase in public income measured in free foreign exchange—that is, the numéraire. Both W_g and W_c are measured in "units," so that ω is a pure number. $\square$

domestic prices accruing to someone at the average level of consumption; that is:

(6) $d = W_c/W_{\bar{c}}$.

$$
\begin{bmatrix}
\textit{Value of private} \\
\textit{sector consumption at} \\
\textit{consumption level c} \\
\textit{relative to that at} \\
\textit{the average level} \\
\textit{of consumption}
\end{bmatrix}
=
\begin{bmatrix}
\textit{Marginal social} \\
\textit{value of private} \\
\textit{sector consumption} \\
\textit{at consumption} \\
\textit{level c}
\end{bmatrix}
\div
\begin{bmatrix}
\textit{Marginal social} \\
\textit{value of} \\
\textit{private sector} \\
\textit{consumption at} \\
\textit{the average level} \\
\textit{of consumption}
\end{bmatrix}
$$

Thus, a marginal increase in consumption at domestic prices accruing to someone enjoying a consumption level c is worth d times as much as a marginal increase in consumption at domestic prices accruing to someone at the average level of consumption.

This discussion was begun by dividing ω into two constituent elements. The elements can now be combined to obtain the final expression for ω. From equations (4), (5), and (6):

$$\omega = W_c/W_g,$$

$$\omega = (W_c/W_{\bar{c}})(W_{\bar{c}}/W_g), \text{ or}$$

(7) $\omega = d/v,$

$$
\begin{bmatrix}
\textit{Value of private} \\
\textit{sector consumption} \\
\textit{at consumption} \\
\textit{level c relative} \\
\textit{to the numéraire}
\end{bmatrix}
=
\begin{bmatrix}
\textit{Value of private} \\
\textit{sector consumption} \\
\textit{at consumption} \\
\textit{level c relative} \\
\textit{to that at the} \\
\textit{average level}
\end{bmatrix}
\div
\begin{bmatrix}
\textit{Value of the} \\
\textit{numéraire relative} \\
\textit{to private sector} \\
\textit{consumption at} \\
\textit{the average level}
\end{bmatrix}
$$

which says that the weight, ω, depends on two factors. The first is d, which is designed to allow for the different values assigned to additional consumption at different existing levels of consumption. This is essentially a pure income distribution parameter. If the government does not wish to use project selection to improve income distribution, d should be set equal to unity. If, however, it does wish to use project selection for this purpose, d will be greater or less than unity depending on whether project-generated income accrues to those enjoying a level of consumption below or above the average level of consumption. The second factor is v, which is designed to allow for the different values assigned to public income (measured in foreign exchange) and private sector consumption (evaluated at the average level of consumption).

It is now possible to substitute into the formula for the social price to obtain the following:

(8)   Social price $=$ Efficiency price $+c(\beta-d/v)$,

$$\begin{bmatrix} Social \\ price \end{bmatrix} = \begin{bmatrix} Efficiency \\ price \end{bmatrix} + \begin{bmatrix} Distributional \\ Impact \end{bmatrix}$$

so that the distributional impact—that is, the increase in private sector consumption—reflects both the cost of the reduction in public income measured in foreign exchange, β, and the social benefit of additional consumption in the private sector, d/v.

The consistent inclusion of distributional considerations in project evaluation will bias project selection according to the value judgments implicit in the distribution weights. For example, if public income is particularly scarce, v will tend to be high, and, in the limit, when v tends to infinity, the transfer of resources from the public sector to the private sector (resulting from the payment of, say, an increase in wages) will be treated as a pure cost so that the social price will exceed the efficiency price by $c\beta$ (see equation [8]). Thus, v reflects the public revenue constraint: in general, the higher v—that is, the scarcer public income—the greater the likelihood that projects will be selected which do not involve a significant transfer of resources from the public sector to private sector consumption. In short, the uses to which public sector income may be put—as, for example, investment in education—are considered more valuable than private sector consumption.

Private sector consumption, however, is not homogeneous: it might be expected that in the eyes of the government the consumption of the poor is more valuable than the consumption of the rich. To allow for this the d parameter is introduced; this, unlike v, is specific to the income recipient. Given the overall constraint on public revenue as indicated by the value of v, the purpose of d is to bias project selection in such a way that the private sector consumption which is generated by project investment will accrue primarily to the poor—or, to put the point differently, factors of production owned by the poor will appear more attractive and project selection will be biased in favor of projects that use such factors. Thus, given the cost of the resource transfer, β, the offsetting social benefit is determined in the light of the overall constraint on public income, v, and the value of providing additional consumption to a particular income class, d. The derivations of d and v are outlined in the next five sections, whose discussion deals with d, the pure distribution parameter, and related matters; and with v, the value of public income, and similar variables. The two subsequent sections illustrate this discussion by means of a simple example; and the two concluding sections of the chapter contain a consideration of intertemporal weights and of the appropriate shadow rate of interest.

CONSUMPTION DISTRIBUTION WEIGHT (*d*)

To derive distribution weights, a utility function must be specified. The basic assumption underlying the utility function is that the utility derived from an increment of consumption is less the higher the existing level of consumption: that is, the marginal utility of consumption decreases as the level of consumption increases. If marginal utility is expressed as U_c, this type of consideration may be formalized as:

(9) $U_c = c^{-n}$,

$$\begin{bmatrix} Marginal\ utility \\ at\ consumption \\ level\ c \end{bmatrix} = \begin{bmatrix} consumption \\ level\ c \end{bmatrix}^{-n}$$

where c is the level of consumption and n is a parameter of the utility function.[8] Although this formula is only one of many that could be used to depict the diminishing nature of marginal utility, this particular formulation has the advantage that n can be given an intuitively appealing meaning: namely, the higher n, the more egalitarian the government's objectives, since the higher n the higher the rate of diminishing marginal utility. For example, if $n=2$ (1), marginal utility is four (two) times higher for a man with a given level of consumption than for a man with a consumption level twice as high. And if $n=0$, the marginal utility of consumption is independent of the level of consumption. For most governments, n would probably center around 1. Values close to zero or 2, although possible, may be considered extreme.

To compare the value of consumption to different people and at different points of time, a point of comparison is needed. For example, the marginal utility of consumption at today's average level of consumption might be chosen; that is, the consumption distribution weight, d, for marginal changes in consumption is:

(10) $d = U_c / U_{\bar{c}} = (\bar{c}/c)^n$,

$$\begin{bmatrix} Consumption \\ distribution \\ weight \\ for\ marginal \\ changes \end{bmatrix} = \begin{bmatrix} Marginal \\ utility\ at \\ consumption \\ level\ c \end{bmatrix} \div \begin{bmatrix} Marginal\ utility \\ at\ average \\ level\ of \\ consumption \end{bmatrix}$$

$$= \begin{bmatrix} Average \\ consumption\ \div\ \ \ \ \ \ \ \\ level \end{bmatrix}^n$$

$$= \begin{bmatrix} Average & Consumption \\ consumption\ \div & level \\ level & c \end{bmatrix}^n$$

8. Total utility, $U(c)$, is obtained by integrating equation (9); that is:

$$U(c) = \frac{1}{1-n} c^{1-n} \text{ if } n \gtrless 1, \text{ and}$$

$$U(c) = \log_e c \text{ if } n = 1. \ \square$$

where the bar indicates average. It follows that the marginal utility of consumption to someone with a level of consumption equal to $2c$ ($0.5\bar{c}$) is 0.5^n (2^n), so that if $n = 2$, marginal utility is $0.25(4)$.

Table 1 illustrates how the value of d changes both with different value judgments—that is, different values for n—and with different existing consumption levels.

With n set equal to zero, as in traditional analytical methods, all additional consumption is considered equally valuable regardless of the recipient's existing level of consumption. As n is increased, so the egalitarian bias is increased: a value of n equal to unity implies quite a pronounced bias in favor of the poor, the weight on additional consumption decreasing proportionately with increases in the existing level of consumption. With n equal to 2, the weight falls with the square of the proportionate increase in the existing consumption level; and, as can be seen from table 1, this leads to a set of weights that implies a marked egalitarian bias. Note that only one such table is required for all countries, because the only information required is the ratio of the existing to the average consumption level, which is a pure number (see the second column in table 1). But for any particular income recipient the relevant value of d may change over time if his consumption level and average consumption are growing at different rates.

It will often be necessary to express nonmarginal increases in consumption relative to the marginal utility of consumption at the average level of consumption: that is, in terms of $\bar{c}^{-n}$. If consumption increases from c_1 to c_2, the increase in utility is $U(c_2) - U(c_1)$, which, in terms of

Table 1. Values of the Consumption Distribution Weight (d) for Marginal Changes in Consumption

		Values of distribution weight (d)				
At existing consumption level (c)	At relative consumption level ($\bar{c}/c$)	And when n equals				
		0	0.5	1.0	1.5	2
10	10.00	1.00	3.16	10.00	31.62	100.00
25	4.00	1.00	2.00	4.00	8.00	16.00
50	2.00	1.00	1.41	2.00	2.83	4.00
75	1.33	1.00	1.15	1.33	1.53	1.77
100 [a]	1.00	1.00	1.00	1.00	1.00	1.00
150	0.66	1.00	0.81	0.66	0.54	0.44
300	0.33	1.00	0.57	0.33	0.19	0.11
600	0.17	1.00	0.41	0.17	0.07	0.03
1,000	0.10	1.00	0.32	0.10	0.03	0.01

a. Average consumption ($\bar{c}$).

the marginal utility of consumption at the average level of consumption, is:

$$\frac{U(c_2) - U(c_1)}{\bar{c}^{-n}}$$

We now want the weight, d, that can be applied directly to $(c_2 - c_1)$ to give the normalized utility value; that is:

$$(c_2 - c_1) d = \frac{U(c_2) - U(c_1)}{\bar{c}^{-n}}; \text{ hence,}$$

(11)
$$d = \frac{U(c_2) - U(c_1)}{(c_2 - c_1)} \Big/ \bar{c}^{-n},$$

$$\begin{bmatrix} Consumption \\ distribution \\ weight\ for \\ nonmarginal \\ changes\ in \\ consumption \end{bmatrix} = \begin{bmatrix} Increase\ in \\ utility \end{bmatrix} \div \begin{bmatrix} Increase\ in \\ consumption \end{bmatrix}$$

$$\div \begin{bmatrix} Marginal\ utility \\ at\ average\ level \\ of\ consumption \end{bmatrix}$$

which formula is the nonmarginal counterpart of equation (10).

Given the form of the utility function, equation (11) can be expressed in n, the basic parameter of the utility function, and two ratios, that of the old to the new level of consumption, c_1/c_2, and that of the average to the new level of consumption, $\bar{c}/c_2$.[9] Table 2 indicates the numerical value of d for different values of n, c_1/c_2, and $\bar{c}/c_2$.[10]

Provided an increase in consumption is intended, $c_1/c_2 < 1$ so that $c_1/c_2 = 0.5$ means that consumption has been doubled; $\bar{c}/c_2$, however, can be ≤ 1. If $\bar{c}/c_2 = 2$ (0.5), consumption has been increased to a level half (twice) as high as average consumption. Thus, assuming $n > 0$, the lower c_1/c_2; and the higher $\bar{c}/c_2$, the higher the weight. This is intuitively acceptable because if c_2 (the new level of consumption) is very much below $\bar{c}$ (the average level of consumption), so that $\bar{c}/c_2$ is high; and if c_1 (the old level of consumption) is very much below c_2 (the new level of consumption) so that c_1/c_2 is small, the increase in consumption is going to someone who is very poor and will in fact still be worse off than the average citizen even after the increase. It presumably would be desirable to attach a high weight to such consumption—which is precisely what the statistics in table 2 indicate. For example, if $\bar{c}/c_2$ is 2 and c_1/c_2 is

9. See "Derivation of d" in the appendix. □
10. As with table 1, table 2 can be used for all countries. □

Table 2. Values of the Consumption Distribution Weight (d) for Nonmarginal Changes in Consumption

		Value of distribution weight (d)				
For ratio of average to new consumption level $(\bar{c}/c_2)$	*For ratio of old to new consumption level* (c_1/c_2)	*And when n equals*				
		0	*0.5*	*1.0*	*1.5*	*2.0*
2	0.25	1.00	1.86	3.70	7.54	16.00
2	0.50	1.00	1.64	2.77	4.69	8.00
2	0.75	1.00	1.47	2.33	3.45	5.30
1	0.25	1.00	1.32	1.85	2.67	4.00
1	0.50	1.00	1.16	1.39	1.66	2.00
1	0.75	1.00	1.04	1.15	1.22	1.30
0.5	0.25	1.00	0.66	0.92	0.92	1.00
0.5	0.50	1.00	0.58	0.69	0.59	0.50
0.5	0.75	1.00	0.52	0.57	0.43	0.33

0.5, then with $n=2$ the value of d is 8. On the other hand, if the consumption accrues to the rich—for example, $\bar{c}/c_2=0.5$ and $c_1/c_2=0.75$ —d will be low, especially if n is high: that is, with $n=2$, $d=0.33$.

SUMMARY DISTRIBUTION MEASURE (D)

Use of the weights in practice requires an estimate of n; this is considered in part III. In addition, the project analyst must obtain information about the beneficiaries of the project. This is already done to some extent, especially in agricultural projects in which the levels of consumption both with, c_2, and without, c_1, the project are reported. That is all the information that the project analyst need collect. The values of $\bar{c}$ and n are not project specific but country specific; hence, they are best provided by the responsible national planning office. The weights can then be determined directly from table 2.

But some effects of the project on consumption may be difficult to trace, too small to bother about, or so general that all income classes would have to be examined. In such cases it is recommended that a *global* distribution weight, D, be used; this is defined as the increase in total welfare generated when an increment in consumption is distributed among the population in the same way as is current aggregate consumption. This definition implies that the increase in consumption has a neutral effect on the distribution of consumption. Accordingly, it might be desirable to assign a slightly higher (lower) value to D if it is thought

Table 3. Values of the Summary Distribution Weight (D)

	Value of summary distribution weight (D)				
For parameter of Pareto distribution function (σ)	*And when n equals*				
	0	*0.5*	*1.0*	*1.5*	*2.0*
1.5	1.0	0.86	1.0	1.3	1.8
2.0	1.0	0.94	1.0	1.1	1.3

that the increase in consumption is improving (worsening) the distribution. A formula for D is derived in the appendix from which table 3 is deduced, where n is the parameter of the utility function, as discussed above, and σ is a parameter of the Pareto distribution function.[11]

As the table illustrates, for $n<1$, D tends to be close to unity. For $n>1$, with the government giving considerable weight to income distribution, plausible values range between 1 and 2, but may be higher for a very high n and low σ.

VALUE OF PUBLIC INCOME (*v*)

To obtain the value of public income relative to the value of additional consumption at the average level of consumption, v, the uses to which it is put must be examined. Given that at the margin public sector income measured in foreign exchange is used for different purposes such as education, defense, consumption subsidies, administration costs, investment, and so on, v may be interpreted as a weighted average of the values of different types of public expenditure, the weights being the proportion of each in the marginal unit of expenditure. If the value of the jth type of expenditure expressed relative to the value of consumption at the average level of consumption is v_j, then:

(12) $\quad v = \sum_j a_j v_j,$

$$
\begin{bmatrix} Value\ of\ num\acute{e}raire \\ relative\ to\ private \\ sector\ consumption \\ at\ the\ average\ level \\ of\ consumption \end{bmatrix} = \sum_j \begin{bmatrix} Proportion\ of\ public \\ expenditure \\ allocated\ to \\ the\ jth\ activity \end{bmatrix} \times \begin{bmatrix} Value\ of\ jth \\ activity\ relative \\ to\ private\ sector \\ consumption\ at \\ the\ average\ level \\ of\ consumption \end{bmatrix}
$$

11. Note that σ is related to the Gini coefficient as follows: Gini coefficient $=1/(2\sigma-1)$. Information on Gini coefficients is available for many countries. □

where a_j equals the proportion of a marginal unit of public income devoted to the jth type of expenditure: that is, $\sum_j a_j = 1$. In principle, all v_j should equal v because a rational government would ensure that at the margin additional expenditure has the same value in all uses. If this is the case, it is necessary only to identify one v_j in order to know the value of v. For example, it might be possible to assess the value of public investment relative to private sector consumption; the resulting value would also be the correct value for v. In practice, however, it is unlikely that the government can secure the equality at the margin of the value of additional expenditure for all purposes, especially because the value of additional expenditure in such sectors as health, defense, and adminis-tration is notoriously difficult to assess. Nevertheless, in the absence of information to the contrary, it may be considered a reasonable working rule to assume that all v_j is approximately equal to v. The following sec-tion contains a discussion of how the value of one particular type of public expenditure might be assessed.

VALUE OF PUBLIC INVESTMENT

In many countries capital expenditure is often treated as a budget-balancing item: if public revenue is scarce (plentiful), it is capital expenditure which suffers (enjoys) the main cutback (expansion). In other words, public investment may be the major component of marginal public expenditure. Its value might be assessed by assuming, for example, that a unit of foreign exchange allocated to public investment produces a stream of output that, measured in foreign exchange, is denoted by q, which is defined as net of the cost required to maintain the unit of capital intact forever. Assume further that q accrues to someone at the average level of consumption, thereby permitting an increase in consumption measured at domestic prices of q/β (β, as defined above, being the relevant ratio of border to domestic prices). If the average level of con-sumption is increasing over time and if diminishing marginal utility is accepted, future consumption must be discounted by a rate that reflects the growth rate of consumption, g, and the rate of diminishing marginal utility, n. Furthermore, if the government considers future consumption less valuable than present consumption simply because it occurs in the future, the discount rate must include an element reflecting pure time preference, ρ. The resulting discount rate, known as the consumption rate of interest (CRI), or social discount rate, i, may be expressed as:

(13) $i = ng + \rho.$[12]

$$\begin{bmatrix} Consumption \\ rate\ of \\ interest \end{bmatrix} = \begin{bmatrix} Parameter \\ of\ utility \\ function \end{bmatrix} \times \begin{bmatrix} Growth\ rate \\ of\ per\ capita \\ consumption \end{bmatrix} + \begin{bmatrix} Rate\ of \\ pure\ time \\ preference \end{bmatrix}$$

The present value of the consumption stream generated by a unit of investment can now be denoted as:

$$v = \sum_{t=0}^{\infty} \frac{q}{\beta(1+i)^t}\ ,\ \text{or}$$

(14) $v = \left[\dfrac{q}{i}\right] \Big/ \beta.$

$$\begin{bmatrix} Value\ of\ num\acute{e}raire \\ relative\ to\ private \\ sector\ consumption \\ at\ the\ average\ level \\ of\ consumption \end{bmatrix} = \begin{bmatrix} Marginal \\ produc- \\ tivity\ of \\ capital \end{bmatrix} \div \begin{bmatrix} Consump- \\ tion \\ rate\ of \\ interest \end{bmatrix}$$

$$\div \begin{bmatrix} Consumption \\ conversion \\ factor \end{bmatrix}$$

Thus, v may be interpreted as the shadow price of public investment (income) relative to a numéraire defined as the marginal utility of consumption at the average level of consumption. Alternatively, a unit of consumption measured at domestic prices accruing to someone at the average level of consumption is worth $1/v (=\beta i/q)$ units of public income measured in foreign exchange, this latter being the chosen numéraire.

Table 4 presents some numerical examples of these relations. The table illustrates the significance of the CRI in determining v; other things being equal, the higher the CRI, the lower v, because future consumption is being discounted more heavily. Noting that the CRI is determined by the growth rate in per capita consumption and by the subjective parameters, n and ρ, it is evident that although the government's preferences concerning income distribution (that is, the ds) are quantified solely by n, its preference for growth (that is, v) is determined jointly by n and ρ. Thus, a high (low) value for n is sufficient to impart a strong (weak) egalitarian bias to project selection, whereas a policy that is heavily growth oriented requires a low CRI, for which both a low ρ and a low n may be necessary.

It should be clear, however, that values for v derived from equation

12. See the appendix for the derivation. □

Table 4. Value of Public Income Relative to Consumption at the Average Level of Consumption (v)

Value of public income relative to consumption at the average level ($v = q/\beta i$)	When parameter of utility function (n) equals	When per capita growth rate (g) equals	When pure time preference (ρ) equals	And hence when consumption rate of interest ($i = ng + \rho$) equals	When marginal product of capital (q) equals	And when consumption conversion factor (β) equals
15.1	1	0.01	0	0.01	0.12	0.8
5.0	1	0.03	0	0.03	0.12	0.8
2.5	1	0.03	0.03	0.06	0.12	0.8
7.5	2	0.01	0	0.02	0.12	0.8
2.5	2	0.03	0	0.06	0.12	0.8
1.7	2	0.03	0.03	0.09	0.12	0.8

(14) are based on many simplifying assumptions. In the appendix a more general formula is provided; it allows for the possibility that the return from investment may be used for different purposes—such as reinvestment, consumption of the poor, or consumption of the rich—and for the possibility that the values of the parameters may change over time. But, as more complications are introduced, the data requirements become excessive. For estimation purposes, therefore, it is necessary either to make simplifications or to seek alternative methods of estimating v.[13]

Whatever method is chosen, it is important that the resulting value of v should not seem implausible in the light of knowledge of government policies in general. One useful test involves computing the critical consumption level at which point public income (measured in foreign exchange) and private consumption (measured in domestic prices at the average level of consumption) are considered equally valuable.[14] In other words, given the value of v derived from some variant of equation (14), it is possible to compute the level of consumption for which the value of d is such that $d/v = \beta$, this being the condition that determines the critical consumption level. For example, if $v = 2.5$ (see table 4), then, with $\beta = 0.8$, d must equal 2.0: that is, $d = v\beta$. From table 1 it is evident that, with $n = 1$, an existing level of consumption equal to one-half the

13. See "Value of Public Income" in chapter ten. □
14. See "Numéraire" in chapter six. □

average level would produce the required value for *d*. Thus, the estimate of *v* implies that the government is indifferent as between additions to its own income and additions to the consumption of those who are currently enjoying one-half the average consumption level. This implication may not seem plausible in the light of other government policies. For example, if the government is providing consumption subsidies to people at the estimated critical consumption level, it might well be argued that the government values additional consumption at this level more highly than its own income, which suggests that *v* has been overestimated. It is only by means of a careful assessment of all the relevant government policies that an acceptable value for *v* can be derived.

VALUE OF PRIVATE SAVINGS

Equation (14) (with the variables appropriately redefined) or some variation thereon should be used to assess the value of private sector investment. Thus far it has been explicitly assumed that additional factor payments lead to additional consumption; more realistically, of course, part will be taxed directly, part will be saved, and part will be consumed. The costs and benefits of the resulting transfer in resources from the public to the private sector now depend not only on the foreign exchange cost of consumption and its social benefit but also on the social costs and benefits of that portion which is saved.

Direct taxation, of course, does not involve a transfer of resources (measured in foreign exchange) from the public to the private sector, because the private sector's disposable income is effectively reduced by the tax payment. Direct taxes should therefore be netted out in determining the social cost or benefit of additional private sector income. Private savings, however, that result either directly or indirectly in private investment will have a foreign exchange cost (that is, the expenditure on investment goods) and a social benefit (the stream of consumption, reinvestment, and taxes generated by the investment). This social benefit of private investment should be evaluated in a manner similar to that employed for public investment.

Some private saving, however, may take the form of an interest-bearing loan to the public sector. Although accruing to the public sector, such saving should not, of course, be considered the equivalent of tax payments, because the former—but not the latter—commits the government to certain obligations: that is, debt servicing. Although in general it may be assumed that public investment is at the expense of alternative marginal public investment, in some cases it may displace private investment—

Table 5. Complete Systems of Distribution Weights for Two Economies

PART A. VALUE OF PUBLIC INCOME RELATIVE TO CONSUMPTION AT THE AVERAGE LEVEL OF CONSUMPTION (v)

Economy	Value of public income relative to consumption at the average level ($v=q/\beta i$)	When parameter of utility function (n) equals	When per capita growth rate (g) equals	When pure time preference (ρ) equals	And hence when consumption rate of interest ($i=ng+\rho$) equals	When marginal product of capital (q) equals	And when consumption conversion factor (β) equals
1	2	0.5	0.01	0.045	0.05	0.08	0.8
2	1.5	2.0	0.04	0.020	0.10	0.10	0.8

PART B. VALUE OF PRIVATE SECTOR CONSUMPTION RELATIVE TO THE NUMÉRAIRE (ω)

At relative consumption level ($\bar{c}/c$)	Value of distribution weight (d) [a]		Value of private sector consumption relative to the numéraire ($\omega=d/v$) [b]	
	In Economy 1	In Economy 2	In Economy 1	In Economy 2
4.00	2.00	16.00	1.00	10.67
2.00	1.41	4.00	0.70	2.67
1.33	1.15	1.77	0.57	1.18
1.00	1.00	1.00	0.50	0.67
0.66	0.81	0.44	0.40	0.29
0.33	0.57	0.11	0.28	0.07
0.17	0.41	0.03	0.20	0.02

a. d is obtained from table 1 using a value of $n = 0.5$ for Economy 1 and $n = 2.0$ for Economy 2.
b. ω is obtained by dividing the values of d by the value of v obtained in part A. For Economy 1, $v = 2$; for Economy 2, 1.5.

in which event the forgone social benefit of the private investment must be assessed to determine the capital cost of the public investment.

EXAMPLES OF COMPLETE SYSTEMS OF DISTRIBUTION WEIGHTS
FOR TWO ECONOMIES

The various threads of the argument can now be brought together in the form of two examples. In Economy 1 per capita consumption levels are very low, and for some time the growth rate of per capita consumption has also been low (1 percent a year) and is expected to remain so in the immediate future. In these circumstances the government of Economy 1, rightly or wrongly, has decided to emphasize growth rather than, but not to the exclusion of, the redistribution of income. As discussed earlier, a relatively mild concern with income distribution implies a low value for n (say, 0.5) and an emphasis on growth requires a low consumption rate of interest (say, 5 percent).[15] The other relevant data for Economy 1 are presented in table 5.

In Economy 2 per capita consumption levels are rising quite quickly (4 percent a year) and are expected to continue to do so, but the distribution of income is becoming increasingly skewed. In line with the government's expressed desire to improve the distribution of income (if necessary, at the expense of some growth), a high value for n (say, 2) and a high consumption rate of interest (say, 10 percent) can be selected.[16] The other relevant data for Economy 2 are presented in table 5. For both economies, v is computed on the assumption that the entire return from investment is consumed (see equation [14]). In the second part of table 5, the weights (the ωs) to be assigned to private sector consumption at different consumption levels are derived. The ds are taken from table 1, and the ωs are then obtained by dividing by v.

The ωs, as defined earlier, are the weights that indicate the value of private sector consumption (measured at domestic prices) in the chosen numéraire, public income (measured in foreign exchange). The figures in table 5 indicate that the greater concern with growth by Economy 1 than Economy 2 is reflected in a relatively low weight for average consumption relative to public income—that is, a weight of 0.50 in Economy

---

15. Given the formula for the consumption rate of interest in equation (13), the implied rate of pure time preference is 4.5 percent for Economy 1. □

16. Given the formula for the consumption rate of interest in equation (13), the implied rate of pure time preference is 2 percent for Economy 2. Thus, Economy 1 displays a higher preference than Economy 2 for projects with quick yields. □

1 compared with 0.67 in Economy 2. On the other hand, the greater concern with income distribution by Economy 2 is reflected in the wider spread of its consumption weights for different relative consumption levels as compared with those for Economy 1.

Thus, the choice of n and ρ affects the determination of the weights in two ways. First, the higher n and ρ—that is, the higher the CRI— the greater will be the discount attached to future consumption and hence the smaller the value of investment (public income) relative to current consumption. Other things being equal, the higher the values for n and ρ, the higher will be the value of the weight assigned to average consumption. Second, the higher n, the greater will be the emphasis on the current redistribution of income. Other things being equal, the higher the value for n, the greater will be the spread of the weights.

This twofold influence of the weights has significant implications for the critical consumption level: that is, the level of private sector consumption at which additional consumption is considered to be as valuable as additional public income. With a high value for the consumption rate of interest (CRI), v can be expected to be small; and with a high value for n, the spread of the ds can be expected to be large. It follows that, though v may be considerably larger than d for relatively high consumption levels, as one moves down the income scale d will increase rapidly so that the critical consumption level, which is determined by the condition $d=v\beta$, will occur at a higher relative consumption level than if v is large (requiring a low value for the CRI) and the spread of the ds is small (requiring a low value for n). Thus, the critical consumption level for Economy 2 (in which CRI$=10$ percent and $n=2$) is 91 percent of the average consumption level, whereas that for Economy 1 (in which CRI$=5$ percent and $n=0.5$) is only 39 percent of the average level. The determination of the critical consumption level in this manner is a useful check on the plausibility of the value for v and the spread of the weights.

Finally, the inclusion of an income distribution objective does not mean that growth is abandoned: even in Economy 2 investment (public income) is worth more than consumption at the average level. On the other hand, growth is not considered to the exclusion of income distribution: even in Economy 1 consumption of the poorest group (those enjoying a consumption level less than 25 percent of the average level) is worth more than public investment. *Consideration of growth and income distribution objectives does not mean the exclusion of either, but it does require a careful specification of the government's preferences in this respect.*

IMPLICATIONS FOR PROJECT SELECTION

The significance of using such a system of weights in project selection can now be examined. The two principal points to keep in mind are, first, that if v is high—that is, if public income is considered very scarce—projects that save or generate public revenue will be favored; and, second, that if the spread of the ds is large—that is, if income distribution is an important objective—projects that benefit the poor rather than the rich will be favored.

It is not possible to draw more precise conclusions about the sectoral allocation of investment that would result from the systematic use of such weights, but generalizations of the following kind can be made: projects that make heavy demands on scarce public funds (such as most infrastructure projects) will be justified only if they charge high prices or other user charges (thereby replenishing the government's coffers) or if they benefit the poor either through employment or price reductions; the justification of projects in the private sector (such as development finance corporations) will be eased to the extent that the government reaps part of the benefits through the fiscal system or the firms have high reinvestment rates. The examples demonstrate that the consistent use of such a system of weights will ensure that the government's revenue position is not eroded and will also bias the selection of projects in favor of those which benefit the poor and against those which benefit the rich. Although it should not be expected that these weights can be estimated with any degree of rigor in practice, it would seem preferable to make rough estimates than to accept traditional analytical practice, which sets all weights equal to unity.

ACCOUNTING RATE OF INTEREST

The choice of numéraire also has implications for the discount rate, because the discount rate is defined as the rate of fall in the value of the numéraire over time. If all values are consistently expressed relative to the numéraire in each period, the discount rate provides the link between different time periods and allows all costs and benefits to be expressed in present value. The rate of fall in the numéraire chosen here—uncommitted public income measured in convertible foreign exchange—is referred to as the accounting rate of interest (ARI). Given the definition of v (see equation [5]) as the value of public income measured in free foreign exchange (that is, W_g) divided by the value of consumption at domestic prices at the average level of consumption ($W_{\bar{c}}$), a relation can be derived between the rates of change of v, W_g, and $W_{\bar{c}}$, or as is discussed in the appendix, between the ARI and the

CRI—but unfortunately this is not helpful as a basis for estimating the ARI.[17] A more promising approach hinges upon the purpose of the ARI, which is to allocate public investment funds to their socially most desirable uses.

If the ARI is set too low, demand for public investment resources will exceed supply, since too many projects will have a positive net present value. If the ARI is set too high, too few projects will pass the test of a positive net present value, and there will be an excess supply of public investment funds. In principle, the ARI should be chosen such that the demand for public investment resources just exhausts the available supply. It follows that the ARI is the internal social rate of return on the marginal project in the public sector. Recalling that q measures the marginal return to public investment measured in free foreign exchange, the ARI can be expressed as:

(15) $\text{ARI} = q - h,$

$$\begin{bmatrix} Accounting \\ rate\ of \\ interest \end{bmatrix} = \begin{bmatrix} Marginal \\ productivity \\ of\ capital \end{bmatrix} - \begin{bmatrix} Distributional \\ impact \end{bmatrix}$$

where h adjusts for the distributional impact of public investment on the private sector. This expression for the social rate of return recalls the basic equation for a social price, with q representing the efficiency price and h representing the distributional impact.[18]

Thus, if public sector investment leads to increased private sector consumption as a result of an increase in the wage bill, h would equal the difference between the social cost of that consumption (in free foreign exchange forgone) and its corresponding social benefit. Only if either the entire return (that is, q) accrues to the government or the costs and benefits of any income accruing to the private sector are exactly offsetting will the ARI equal capital's marginal product (the traditional discount rate).

TRADITIONAL ANALYTICAL PRACTICE

Traditional practice rests on either of two assumptions. The first is that the fiscal system is able to redistribute income to the extent necessary to make, at the margin, the cost, β, and benefit, d/v, of each distributional impact approximately equal. Project selection should then

17. Thus, the ARI is the rate of change of W_g over time and the CRI is the rate of change of $W_{\bar{z}}$ over time. □
18. See "Efficiency and Social Prices" in chapter six. □

aim to maximize aggregate income, and project analysis need be concerned only with efficiency prices.[19]

If this is not an acceptable assumption, it is necessary to resort to the other assumption: that the government is indifferent to the distribution of project benefits both between different consumers and between consumption and investment, so that once more the maximization of aggregate income is the appropriate objective for project selection. The value judgments implicit in this procedure are, first, that n equals zero, thereby removing the need for the pure income distribution weight (that is, all $d=1$, as shown in table 1); and, second, that ρ (the rate of pure time preference) equals q, thereby ensuring that the value of a marginal increase in private consumption $(1/v)$ exactly equals its cost in forgone public income (β).[20] In words, the approach implies a zero rate of diminishing marginal utility $(n=0)$ and a rate of pure time preference equal to the opportunity cost of capital $(\rho=q)$. Thus, traditional analytical practice may be viewed as a special case of the more general methodology outlined here. Other special cases are also covered,[21] but none of these, including that traditionally employed by the World Bank and other institutions, should be accepted without careful consideration and justification. □

19. With a large project, it would be necessary to change taxes simultaneously to ensure that all the weights $(\beta-d/v)$ remain zero. □

20. From equation (14) the required condition is $i=q$; but, given $n=0$, this becomes $\rho=q$; $1/v$ then equals β. □

21. For example, if the government is not interested in the interpersonal distribution of consumption but is anxious to increase investment, the relevant assumptions are $n=0$ (so that $d=1$ for all consumers) and $\rho<q$ (so that the social benefit of increased consumption is less than its cost in forgone public income). In this version, benefits that are consumed will receive a lower weight than benefits that are invested or that accrue to the public sector, but there will be no differentiation of benefits among consumers. □

CHAPTER EIGHT

Shadow Wage Rates

THUS FAR, IT HAS BEEN SHOWN how weights may be calculated that reflect the basic subjective tradeoff between growth and income distribution. This process, however, is only part of the task of estimating shadow prices, and in this section we cover the other elements of the shadow price: the forgone output or opportunity cost and the increase in income (if any) accruing to the factor of production. As an illustration we consider the shadow wage rate, but the principle is completely generalizable.

One point must be stressed at the outset: shadow prices for labor will vary considerably depending on such factors as skill and location. We shall discuss these factors in general and conclude with a specific illustration of one particular shadow wage rate formula that, despite this variation, may have a fairly wide application.

FORGONE OUTPUT

The use of labor in a project prevents its use elsewhere. The forgone output of this labor in its best alternative use is a major component of the social cost of using that labor, since productive efficiency is presumably a basic objective of policy. We need, therefore, an estimate of output forgone. If the market for the type of labor concerned is reasonably efficient, then the market wage gives a good measure of the marginal product of that labor at market prices, m,[1] as well as the forgone output.

In general, this is a good approach for estimating the forgone output of skilled labor, and labor markets for unskilled labor may also be sufficiently active, even in rural areas, to permit the use of this method. Unskilled labor may be drawn from family farms (as is often the case in rural areas), but it is still acceptable to estimate its marginal product by the going (rural) wage rate provided that the labor market is fairly active and that, at the margin, the family farms generally participate in that market.

---

1. For a definition of all symbols, see the glossary of symbols on page 149. □

Note here that the relevant labor market and wage is not where the labor is to be employed but where it comes from. If rural labor is drawn into industrial employment, with industrial wages well above rural ones, the question is whether rural wages form an acceptable measure of output forgone; the higher industrial wage may or may not reflect labor's marginal product in industry, but it is certainly no yardstick of labor's marginal product in agriculture. In all these cases, the estimate of labor output forgone at market prices may need further adjustment by means of an accounting ratio, α, to obtain its value at border prices.[2]

This estimation procedure relies on the equality, first, of the forgone output and labor's marginal product, and, second, of the marginal product and the market wage. This approach is not always suitable or feasible. For example, if more than one rural worker migrates to the urban sector in response to the creation of only one job in that sector, the forgone output will be greater than one worker's marginal product. Whether this is a serious complication is as yet a moot question. For the many projects situated in rural areas, the problem probably does not arise; but if there is good reason to believe that an urban project will have an excess-migration effect, some attempt should be made to assess its cost.

If the relevant labor market is imperfect, the forgone output should not be equated with the market wage concerned. Imperfect markets may often be encountered in rural areas, especially during slack agricultural seasons. Frequently, the market wage will be above the supply price of labor—that is, the wage at which labor is willing to work [3]— which implies that a labor surplus exists in the area. Output forgone in employing workers from such an area is less than the market wages prevailing there—but output forgone is not necessarily zero. For example, the theoretically unemployed worker may occupy himself with some form of self-employment, such as house repair or fishing. Even if there is no forgone output at all during the slack season, it may be expected that the labor force will be more or less fully employed during the peak agricultural season.

2. For some categories of labor, especially semiskilled and skilled labor, it may not always be possible to identify the nature of the forgone output even though it is safe to assume that the market wage paid, both in the project and elsewhere, is a good measure of the market value of the forgone output. In other words, it may not always be possible to identify the appropriate accounting ratio, in which case it will be necessary to resort to a "standard conversion factor." See "Standard Conversion Factor" in chapter nine. □

3. This is discussed further in "Disutility of Effort," below. Here, concern is only with forgone output. □

In determining forgone output and hence the cost of labor, it is necessary, therefore, to specify the season(s) for which the labor is required. Moreover, the labor surplus may disappear over time, especially if the area experiences a reasonable rate of economic development. Hence, if the labor is required for a project lasting twenty years, it may be misleading to assume that currently surplus labor will have a zero forgone output over the entire life of the project. This situation represents one aspect of the general problem of predicting future prices for the purpose of project analysis.

In some rural areas, of course, there is no labor market. On family farms that do not hire or hire out workers, labor will be employed up to the point at which the marginal product equals the disutility of extra work: that is, the value of forgone leisure. Removing one worker will mean an immediate loss of output equal to the worker's marginal product. But, assuming diminishing returns, the removal of one worker will increase the marginal product of the remaining members of the family, who will therefore increase their work input up to the point at which marginal product again equals marginal disutility of effort. If this marginal disutility is constant over the relevant range of hours worked per man, the net effect on output will be zero. On the other hand, if the marginal disutility rises sharply with extra work, the remaining family members will hardly increase their working hours, and the net forgone output will approximately equal the marginal product of the removed worker. In general the forgone output will be somewhere between zero and labor's marginal product.[4]

DISUTILITY OF EFFORT

A new job frequently calls for an increase in effort on the part of the worker, either because he has to work more hours or because the work is more arduous. The disutility of this increased effort can be measured by the difference between labor's supply price for the new and the old jobs. This supply price is the wage that must be paid to induce the worker into a particular employment and reflects the worker's private evaluation of all its aspects, pleasant and unpleasant. In a perfect labor market, the supply price of labor equals the market wage. In imperfect

4. Note that similar complications arise, even with a perfect labor market, if the project's demand for labor is so large as to affect the wage level. Output forgone in that case depends on the elasticity of labor response to higher wages in the area. Wages are then not a good measure of output forgone. Compare the discussion of accounting prices in "Commodity Prices" in the appendix. □

markets, however, the market wage will exceed labor's supply price, so that wage differences are a poor guide to differences in supply prices for different occupations. This may often be the case in less developed countries, especially with respect to the transfer of labor from the rural to the urban sector. In such cases a direct assessment must be made of any disutility of effort that may be involved in a new job. For labor on family farms in an area without an active labor market changes in marginal labor product provide a rough estimate of changes in supply price and increased effort, as noted above.

Finally, the supply price of an unemployed man is not necessarily zero. There is considerable evidence that unemployed labor cannot be tempted into employment below a (subsistence) wage of three kilograms' grain-equivalent a day. In some cases it may be possible to ascertain the specific minimum, or reservation, wage necessary to activate the unemployed in any particular area; otherwise this more or less universal subsistence figure may be used.

Crude estimates of the disutility of increased effort probably suffice in practice. For example, if the labor for a project is drawn from full-time employment, it is often reasonable to assume that there is no increased effort involved. For previously unemployed labor, a rough estimate of the reservation wage will give an acceptable measure of the disutility of effort. Where more information is available, the estimates can be improved. The resulting value will be a measure of the private cost of increased effort relative to the additional income that is required just to offset that increased effort.

The government, however, may not regard the private cost of increased effort as an accurate measure of its social cost.[5] In some cases the additional income received may more than offset the increased effort. Let e be the ratio of the wage earner's own evaluation of the disutility of effort to his additional income, and ϕ be the ratio of the social to the private evaluation of the disutility of effort. Then the social cost per unit of additional income is ϕe. If the government costs increased effort in the same way as does the private individual, then $\phi = 1$. But in its desire for development narrowly interpreted as increased consumption, the government may not consider increased effort as a

5. Note that, given a welfare function that includes only consumption, it is not strictly correct to introduce the disutility of effort or the value of leisure into the shadow wage rate. Theoretically, it would be necessary to redefine the welfare function to include leisure and then to deduce a new set of shadow prices. It might be expected, however, that the shadow wage rate would be the only price affected to any significant extent. □

cost, in which case $\phi = 0$. Intermediate values can also be used. If $e = 1$, the increased income for the wage earner is exactly offset by the increased effort; if $e = 0$, there is no private cost of increased effort.

CHANGES IN INCOME

Employment on the project frequently involves changes in income, especially if the labor is drawn from the rural sector. But since a shift in employment of industrial-skilled workers does not in general result in increased labor income, the following discussion applies principally to unskilled rural labor.

The transfer of one worker from rural unemployment or underemployment to full-time employment on a project has different effects on income depending on whence he comes. If the labor is drawn directly or indirectly from an area with an efficient labor market, the increase in income will equal the difference between the new wage and the wage in the alternative employment. If the laborer is landless, this increase in income will accrue solely to him: if the wage in the new job is w, the increase in his income is $w - m$, where m is the marginal product in his previous employment that, in an efficient labor market, equals the rural wage. For farm family labor, however, part of the increase in income may accrue to the transferred worker's family; and for labor transferring from the rural to the urban sector, part of the increase in income may be offset by higher prices and other increased living costs.[6]

The changes in income should be adjusted to obtain their social cost or benefit. This will depend on the proportions consumed and saved and on the disutility of effort. For simplicity, assume that private savings are considered as socially valuable as public income [7] so that both saving and any direct taxation can be netted out. Assume that the remaining portion, c, of the initial increase in income is spent on a basket of commodities for which the relevant accounting ratio is β. Thus, the foreign exchange cost of the increased consumption is βc. The social benefit of this consumption may be assessed as follows. If leisure is treated as a consumption good, the private value of the increase in consumption is $c(1 - e)$, where e is the ratio of the private value of forgone leisure to the market value of increased consumption. Two adjustments are required to obtain the social value of this consumption: first, e must be adjusted to reflect the social value of forgone leisure; and, second, the resulting value of consumption, $c(1 - \phi e)$, must

6. See "Price Indexes" in chapter twelve. □
7. See, however, "Value of Private Savings" in chapter seven. □

be weighted by the relevant ω, or d/v. Thus, a social value is obtained for the increased consumption of $c(1-\phi e)\omega$, as well as a net social cost of $c[\beta-(1-\phi e)\omega]$. The numerical implications of this result are examined in the following two sections.

A SHADOW WAGE RATE FORMULA

The various elements of the shadow wage rate (SWR) can now be inserted into the basic formula for the social price, which was written earlier as social price = efficiency price + $c(\beta-\omega)$. The efficiency price, or opportunity cost of labor, has been discussed earlier, as have change in income and β and ω. In the case of the SWR there is an additional element in the form of the disutility of increased effort. From the foregoing discussion it should be apparent that the various elements of the formula depend on the type of labor: that is, an SWR must be estimated for each particular type of labor.

Consider the case of an unskilled worker being drawn from a perfect labor market into employment that pays a fixed wage, w, that exceeds the forgone marginal product, m. If the worker consumes the entire increase in income:

(16) $\text{SWR} = m\alpha + (w-m)(\beta-d/v) + (w-m)\phi ed/v$,

$$\begin{bmatrix} Shadow \\ wage \\ rate \end{bmatrix} = \begin{bmatrix} Labor's\ forgone \\ marginal\ prod- \\ uct\ at\ account- \\ ing\ prices \end{bmatrix} + \begin{bmatrix} Net\ social\ cost \\ of\ increased \\ consumption \end{bmatrix} + \begin{bmatrix} Social\ cost \\ of\ reduced \\ leisure \end{bmatrix}$$

where $m\alpha$ is the forgone output measured at border prices (the efficiency price of labor); $(\hat{w}-m)$ is the increase in consumption (measured at market prices) that is multiplied by an accounting ratio, β, to obtain the cost to the government in terms of forgone foreign exchange and by weights d/v and $\phi ed/v$ that reflect the social value of increased consumption and the social cost of reduced leisure.

It is useful to consider further the implications of certain critical values of the parameters or of certain simplifying assumptions that may be appropriate.

First, set $d/v=\beta$ (that is, the government is indifferent about the distribution of income as between the private and public sectors) and set $\phi=0$ (that is, the social cost of increased effort is zero); then:

(17) $\text{SWR} = m\alpha$.

$$\begin{bmatrix} Shadow \\ wage \\ rate \end{bmatrix} = \begin{bmatrix} Labor's\ forgone \\ marginal\ product \\ at\ accounting\ prices \end{bmatrix}$$

This SWR measures only forgone output at accounting prices and is a good starting place for the examination of alternative assumptions.

Second, let $v \to \infty$ (that is, the government does not value private sector consumption); then:

(18) $SWR = m\alpha + (w - m)\beta.$

$$\begin{bmatrix} Shadow \\ wage \\ rate \end{bmatrix} = \begin{bmatrix} Labor's\ forgone \\ marginal\ product \\ at\ accounting\ prices \end{bmatrix} + \begin{bmatrix} Gross\ social \\ cost\ of\ increased \\ consumption \end{bmatrix}$$

This SWR would be appropriate if the government's sole aim is to maximize growth. Equation (18) can be rewritten as:

$$SWR = w\beta + (\alpha - \beta)m.$$

The factor $(\alpha - \beta)$ adjusts the marginal product so that it reflects accounting rather than market prices.[8] α is applied to m when m is viewed as output: β is applied to m when m is viewed as consumption goods bought with the income represented by m. If $\alpha = \beta$, then the $SWR = w\beta$: that is, the consumption cost of the market wage paid on the project at accounting prices.

Third, set d and v equal to specific values based on the country's income distribution and growth objectives and set $\phi = 0$; then:

(19) $SWR = m\alpha + (w - m)(\beta - d/v).$

$$\begin{bmatrix} Shadow \\ wage \\ rate \end{bmatrix} = \begin{bmatrix} Labor's\ forgone \\ marginal\ product \\ at\ accounting\ prices \end{bmatrix} + \begin{bmatrix} Net\ social \\ cost\ of\ increased \\ consumption \end{bmatrix}$$

This SWR is appropriate if the government's objectives include growth and income redistribution. The SWR will be higher the more important the growth objective (that is, the higher v) and lower the more important the income redistribution objective and the poorer the income recipient (that is, the higher d).

Fourth, set d and v equal to specific values and set $\phi = 1$; then:

(20) $SWR = m\alpha + (w - m)(\beta - d/v) + (w - m)ed/v.$

$$\begin{bmatrix} Shadow \\ wage \\ rate \end{bmatrix} = \begin{bmatrix} Labor's\ forgone \\ marginal\ prod- \\ uct\ at\ account- \\ ing\ prices \end{bmatrix} + \begin{bmatrix} Net\ social \\ cost\ of \\ increased \\ consumption \end{bmatrix} + \begin{bmatrix} Social\ cost \\ of\ reduced \\ leisure\ for \\ \phi = 1 \end{bmatrix}$$

This SWR considers the social cost of private effort on a par with other costs and benefits. The SWR will be lower if ϕ is set at a level less than

8. See chapter nine. □

unity, reflecting a judgment that the government considers increased private effort less of a cost than output forgone or consumption.

In the past, economic appraisals of projects have usually assumed that the SWR equals the forgone marginal output at market prices: that is, that SWR$=m$. In other words, the implicit assumptions have been:

—That the government does not regard increased effort as a social cost, so that $\phi=0$;
—That the distribution of consumption is considered optimal or that the government does not wish to use project selection to influence the existing distribution, so that $d=1$;
—That public income is considered as valuable as private consumption, when both are measured in foreign exchange, so that $v=1/\beta$;
—That the market price of the forgone output reflects the social value of that output, so that $\alpha=1$; and
—That the forgone output equals labor's marginal product.

NUMERICAL EXAMPLE OF THE SHADOW WAGE RATE FORMULA

Assume the following best estimates of the parameters required for the SWR given by equation (16): $m/w=0.5$; $\bar{c}/w=1.0$; $e=0.5$; $\alpha=0.9$; $\beta=0.8$; $n=1$; $\phi=0.5$; and $v=3$—where $\bar{c}$ is the average per capita consumption level. If the wage is supporting more than one person, it should be transformed into per capita terms, which is the relevant concept for comparison with $\bar{c}$. Given the value of n and the ratios $\bar{c}/w$ and m/w, the distribution parameter, d, can be determined from table 2.[9] The value of v implies that public income is considered three times as valuable as average consumption. The formulas above give the following alternative SWR estimates:

From equation (17):
  SWR$=0.5\times0.9w=0.45w$.
From equation (18):
  SWR$=(0.45+0.5\times0.8)w=0.85w$.
From equation (19):
  SWR$=(0.85-0.5\times1.4/3)w=0.62w$.

9. The value of d is taken from table 2 using values of $c_1=m$ and $c_2=w$. If leisure is viewed as a consumption commodity, the distribution weight, d, strictly speaking should be derived from table 2 for values of c_1, c_2, and $\bar{c}$ that include the value of leisure associated with these consumption levels. This complication is not considered in the remainder of this section. □

From equation (20):
$$SWR = (0.62 + 0.5 \times 0.5 \times 1.4/3)w = 0.74w.$$
From equation (16):
$$SWR = (0.62 + 0.5 \times 0.5 \times 0.5 \times 1.4/3)w = 0.68w.$$

In this particular example the smallest SWR occurs when only forgone output is considered (equation [17])—the traditional analytical approach. If the increased consumption is then treated as a pure cost (equation [18]), the maximum SWR is obtained. The recognition that consumption does have some value (equation [19]) reduces the SWR, but the inclusion of the disutility of effort (equation [20]) again raises the SWR. Finally, if the government costs only part of the disutility of effort (equation [16]) a somewhat lower SWR is attained.[10]

OTHER FACTOR INCOMES

The discussion of the SWR showed how the increased consumption out of wage income generated by employment should be weighted to reflect both its foreign exchange cost to the government and its social value either as consumption or savings. All increases in income attributable to the project—from profits, rents, consumer surplus, and so on—should be treated in a similar manner, but four points should be borne in mind. First, the value of d will vary with the level of the individual's consumption. For example, it might be appropriate to attach a high weight if the increased consumption accrues to peasant farmers and a very low weight if it takes the form of profits paid out to the rich. Second, only increases in income should be considered. For example, if it is reasonable to assume that a rentier will receive the same interest payment wherever he invests his capital, then investing in a government project will not imply any increase in income and hence consumption or savings.

Third, some increases in income may appear on the cost side and some may appear on the benefit side. In the shadow wage rate example above, the increased income was included on the cost side. If, however, it were to be transferred to the benefit side, merely a change in sign would be required. In other words, the numerical value of the weight is not affected by the transfer, but the sign must be changed.

Fourth, note that distributional weights are not applied to the output

10. It is quite possible to obtain an SWR that is lower than labor's forgone output, especially if the labor involved remains poor even after the increase in income: that is, if $c_2 < \bar{c}$. □

or sales generated by the project, but only to the increases in income to which the project gives rise. In other words, the benefits of a project are not greater because its output is sold to the poor rather than the rich (unless sales to the poor involve subsidies, or income transfers); what matters is whether their consumption (income) increases because of the project.

CONSUMER SURPLUS

Consumer surplus is usually defined as the area below the demand curve and above the price line. A reduction in the price of a commodity causes an immediate gain to consumers represented by the quantity they consume times the price reduction. In addition, the price reduction may also induce consumers to buy more of the commodity, which will again lead to an increase in consumer surplus (that is, the small consumer surplus triangle). The total increase in consumer surplus should be treated as a benefit, and, as such, it must be weighted by the appropriate d/v so it can be expressed in terms of the chosen numéraire.

The reallocation of expenditure may also involve a foreign exchange cost or benefit, depending on whether the elasticity of demand is less or greater than unity. If the elasticity is less (greater) than unity, the reduction in price will reduce (increase) expenditure on that commodity, thereby increasing (reducing) the consumption—and thus the foreign exchange cost—of other commodities. The foreign exchange cost of the commodity whose price has been reduced is not included, because generally this commodity will be the output of the project, and hence its costs of production will appear as project costs. □

CHAPTER NINE

Accounting Prices for Traded and Nontraded Commodities

IT IS CONVENIENT to distinguish four categories of commodities: [1]

—Commodities that, at the margin, are being imported (exported) and for which the elasticity of world supply (demand) is infinite;

—Commodities that, at the margin, are being imported (exported) and for which the elasticity of world supply (demand) is less than infinite;

—Commodities that are not currently being traded but that ought to be traded if the country adopted optimal trade policies; and

—Commodities that are not currently being traded and ought not to be traded even if the country adopted optimal trade policies.

Each category will be discussed in turn.

TRADABLES SUBJECT TO INFINITE ELASTICITIES

Imported commodities falling in the first category, above, should be valued, or costed, at the c.i.f. border price plus the relevant marketing margin revalued at accounting prices. Similarly, exported commodities falling in this category should be valued, or costed, at the f.o.b. price minus the relevant marketing margin revalued at accounting prices. [2]

The rationale of this treatment is straightforward. The impact of an increased demand for, or increased supply of, such commodities is solely on trade. The infinite elasticity assumption ensures that domestic prices and hence domestic consumption and production remain unchanged. Thus, the production of imports (that is, import substitution) or exports (export promotion) increases the availability of foreign exchange by an

---

1. The term "commodities" should be interpreted in a broad sense to include services as well as commodities proper. □

2. The revaluation of the marketing margins is an aspect of the general revaluation of nontraded commodities and will be discussed below. It is recommended that the marketing margins be kept separate and then be converted en bloc into accounting prices at the end of the exercise. □

amount equal to the quantity produced times the relevant border price. Projects that demand imports or exports have the reverse effect.

It is important to note three points concerning the use of border prices. First, project demand may be supplied by domestic sources rather than imports. But provided the local and imported product are equivalent [3] and provided the elasticity of foreign supply is infinite, then, at the margin the impact will still be on trade because other domestic users will now have to switch from domestic supplies to imported supplies. Second, the use of border prices implies that commodities are valued, or costed, directly in relation to the chosen numéraire: uncommitted public income measured in foreign exchange.[4] (This is an additional reason for the selection of this particular numéraire.) Third, the use of border prices does not require the assumption of free trade; for example, a commodity subject to a high import tariff should still be valued, or costed, at its c.i.f. price provided it is imported (that is, the tariff is not prohibitive) and provided the elasticity of foreign supply is infinite (that is, domestic prices are not affected).

TRADABLES SUBJECT TO FINITE ELASTICITIES

If a project causes an increase in the demand for, or supply of, commodities falling in the second category, above, there will be a change in the border price that will have repercussions on domestic consumers and producers. Most less developed countries are too small to influence the border prices of importables, so the following discussion relates to an increase in supply of an exportable for which the world demand is less than perfectly elastic.

In this case it is still necessary to establish the relation between the border and domestic price, but in principle a further adjustment is now required to allow for the transfers of income caused by the price change and the effects on foreign exchange. This includes the social value and (foreign exchange) cost of changes in producer and consumer income— plus the foreign exchange effects of a lower price for existing exports and of switches in domestic production and consumption. In practice, it may be sufficiently accurate to consider only the direct foreign exchange effect and to ignore the income transfers and substitution effects.

3. Formally, the condition for perfect substitutes is infinite cross-elasticities of demand. □

4. As discussed earlier, the numéraire and therefore the border prices are expressed in units of the domestic currency, converted at the official exchange rate. □

The appropriate accounting price is then the marginal export revenue, which may be expressed as the border price multiplied by $(1-1/\eta)$, where η is the elasticity of foreign demand defined so as to be positive.[5] By analogy, the appropriate accounting price for an importable is the marginal import cost, which may be expressed as the border price multiplied by $(1+1/\epsilon)$, where ϵ is the elasticity of foreign supply.[6]

POTENTIALLY TRADED COMMODITIES

The third category, above, includes commodities that are not currently being traded but which ought to be traded if the country adopted optimal trade policies. This category includes the outputs of industries that produce behind prohibitive tariffs or quotas and for which the marginal cost (at accounting prices) of increasing domestic production exceeds the cost of importing. In the evaluation of projects that use inputs supplied by such industries, the evaluator faces a dilemma. On the one hand, he does not want to jeopardize the project by pricing the input at the marginal cost of inefficient domestic production when, in the absence of the protective barrier, the input could be imported at a much lower cost; on the other hand, he does not want to use the (relatively) low border price if in fact the input will be supplied by a high-cost domestic producer.

The solution is to predict the actual source of supply and to price the input according to the cost of that supply. The presumption, however, should be that the predicted supplier will be the lowest cost supplier, and that the government can be persuaded to lower the prohibitive tariff (or remove the quota) so that at the margin the input is actually imported.[7] If such broad action proves impossible, the government may be persuaded to grant to the project alone this access to imports, thereby making the input an importable for the purposes of the evaluation. If, despite all efforts, it is clear that the project will be supplied by the high-cost domestic producer, the input should be regarded as a nontradable (that is, falling in the fourth category of commodities).

---

5. If foreign demand is perfectly elastic—that is, if $\eta \to \infty$—the correct accounting price is the border price, as prescribed for commodities falling in the first category, above. For a definition of symbols, see the glossary of symbols. □

6. If foreign supply is perfectly elastic—that is, if $\epsilon \to \infty$—the correct accounting price is the border price, as prescribed for commodities falling in the first category, above. □

7. What matters is not whether the project imports its inputs, but whether the demand from the project leads to additional imports to meet the increase in domestic demand. □

Production, however, may take place behind a high tariff, while at the margin additional demand—for example, for the project—is met by imports; the inputs should then be treated as traded.

There is one important exception to this general prescription. Some industries are afforded temporary protection during their early development, while their efficiency is being increased to a level that will permit them to compete successfully against imports. Such industries should be encouraged. It is recommended, therefore, that if an infant industry is clearly identifiable, project demand should be supplied by that industry—but the input should be costed at its border price in order not to jeopardize the project being evaluated. Caution should be exercised, however, in deciding whether a protected industry can be considered in its infancy. Import substitution industries in many cases never become competitive with imports; each case must be examined on its merits.

Similar comments apply to the valuation of a project's output that, although potentially importable, is not currently being imported at the margin because of high import tariffs or quotas. Every effort should be made to persuade the government to remove the protective barrier (unless the infant industry argument applies) so that the output can be treated as a tradable. If this fails, the output should be regarded as a nontradable and valued accordingly, as discussed below. In such cases it is a useful additional exercise to evaluate the project as though its output were tradable. If the project is still profitable when the output is valued on the basis of the c.i.f. price, then the project will survive even if at some future date the protective barrier is removed. If the project is not profitable at border prices, the excess cost of domestic production (properly assessed) over the cost of imports measures the cost of retaining the protective barrier. The government should be made fully aware of the cost that will be incurred if they proceed with the project rather than lower the protective barrier to permit imports.

NONTRADED COMMODITIES

Nontraded commodities, the fourth category, are defined as having a domestic supply price, at the given level of local demand, below the c.i.f. price of imports but above the f.o.b. price of exports.[8] Depending on the elasticities of supply and demand, an increase in demand for nontraded goods as a consequence of the project will be satisfied by decreased con-

---

8. This definition should also include commodities that are potentially tradable but actually nontraded because of trade barriers. □

sumption elsewhere in the economy or by increased production. If the main source of supply is increased domestic production, without a significant price increase, it is recommended that the accounting price be interpreted as the marginal social cost of increased production. Alternatively, if the main source of supply is reduced consumption elsewhere, with a significant price increase, it is recommended that the accounting price be interpreted as the forgone marginal social benefit in consumption. In the long run it may be reasonable to assume that demand is met primarily by increased production; but in the short run the supply, especially for capital-intensive nontraded goods, may be relatively fixed.

ESTIMATION OF MARGINAL SOCIAL COST

The marginal social cost of a nontraded good is determined as follows: decompose the nontraded good into its constituent inputs and value each input at its accounting price. Some of these inputs will be traded commodities with shadow prices determined in the manner described above; others will be primary factors, with shadow prices determined in the manner described for labor.[9] The remaining inputs will themselves be nontraded, and they in turn must be evaluated through a further round of decomposition until eventually everything is decomposed into traded goods and primary factors. The degree of sophistication required will depend on the case in hand and the availability of time and data.

ESTIMATION OF MARGINAL SOCIAL BENEFIT

If demand is met by decreasing consumption elsewhere, the accounting price is the marginal social benefit that can be calculated by observing the benefits forgone as a result of project demand. For intermediates, an estimate of the social profit forgone is desirable, and, for commodities entering final consumption, an estimate of the loss in consumer surplus appropriately revalued in terms of the numéraire is desirable. In addition, for both types of commodity allowances should be made for any reallocation of expenditure induced by the price rise. Only if the elasticity of demand is unity—that is, total expenditure on the commodity both before and after the price rise is the same—will this effect be zero. If the elasticity is less (greater) than unity, the price increase will increase (reduce) expenditure on the commodity, thereby reducing (increasing) the foreign exchange cost of expenditure on other commodities. Finally, the price

---

9. See chapter eight. □

increase will cause a transfer of income from consumers to producers equal to the original quantity demanded times the change in price. The social cost-benefit of this transfer will depend on the weights appropriate to the income groups involved. These weights, discussed in chapter seven, must be estimated in the manner described in chapter ten. If it is thought that, in general, producers are richer than consumers, the net effect of the transfer would constitute a social cost, but if producers and consumers are indistinguishable, it will be reasonable to assume that the transfer has a zero net social cost.

STANDARD CONVERSION FACTOR

Although in general it is recommended that a different accounting price be estimated for different nontraded goods, it is useful to have available a standard conversion factor that can be used for minor nontraded items or for the nontraded goods which remain after one or two rounds of decomposition. For this purpose, the ratio of the value at border prices of all exports and imports to their value at domestic prices might be used.[10] As such, the SCF bears a close relation to the more familiar concept of the shadow exchange rate (SER). The precise relation is:

(21)   SCF/OER = 1/SER,

$$\begin{bmatrix} Standard \\ conversion \\ factor \end{bmatrix} \div \begin{bmatrix} Official \\ exchange \\ rate \end{bmatrix} = \begin{bmatrix} Inverse\ of \\ shadow \\ exchange\ rate \end{bmatrix}$$

where OER is the official exchange rate. Thus, the SCF translates domestic prices into border prices expressed in units of the domestic currency, and division by the OER expresses the result in units of foreign exchange. The SER combines these two steps.[11]

DEPENDENCE ON POLICY ASSUMPTIONS

Shadow prices are sensitive to the assumptions made about the future development of the economy and, in particular, of trade policy. Changes

10. Imports subject to fixed quotas should be treated as nontradables, provided that the quotas are already fully used and are not expected to be relaxed in the near future. □

11. Note that β, the ratio of the value of a basket of consumption goods at border prices to its value at domestic prices, may also be interpreted as the accounting ratio for a nontraded item (that is, consumption). Therefore, with some loss of accuracy, it is possible to use the SCF for all consumption baskets rather than to estimate individual βs. See "Derivation of β" in chapter seven. □

in tariffs, in quota restrictions, and in the exchange rate will affect the accounting ratios and the remuneration of primary factors as relative (domestic) prices change and resources are reallocated. The range of possible policy scenarios is obviously large. Only two (extreme) alternatives are considered here to illustrate the considerations that should be borne in mind in adjusting shadow prices to expected policy developments.

In the first policy scenario the country is faced with a balance-of-payments deficit caused by "living beyond one's means," and domestic factor prices are inflexible in nominal terms. If, to cope with this situation, a devaluation is foreseen, it may be appropriate to recalculate some of the shadow prices. Real wages will be reduced in the sense that a fixed money wage can now purchase fewer traded commodities, thereby securing an immediate improvement in the balance of payments.[12] In addition, there may be a reduction in the prices of domestic resources (especially labor) relative to those for traded goods, a circumstance that will further improve the balance of payments by making nontraded commodities more attractive (in both production and consumption) relative to traded items. These changes are reflected in the shadow prices. Thus, the shadow wage rate will decrease relative to the accounting prices of traded goods: the latter remain approximately constant relative to the real numéraire currency,[13] but only some elements of the shadow wage rate (such as m) are fixed in physical terms and hence relative to the real numéraire, whereas other elements (such as w) are fixed in terms of nominal domestic currency by assumption and hence decline in terms of the real numéraire. Similarly, the marginal social cost of nontradables will decrease relative to the price of tradables because, although some of the inputs will be tradables, other inputs will be domestic resources such as labor. The information required to trace through these effects is formidable, and in

---

12. These comments do not apply to the type of economy that is experiencing successive rounds of exchange rate devaluation and domestic price inflation. As a first approximation, it might be assumed that in such an economy the real exchange rate is constant. □

13. If the border prices of traded goods, expressed in units of foreign currency, remain constant, border prices in units of the local currency will increase proportionately to the rate of devaluation. Furthermore, if the appropriate price deflator used to maintain the real value of the numéraire, which is expressed in units of local currency, is based only on traded goods, this deflator will also be proportionate to the rate of devaluation. Only in that case would the accounting prices of traded goods remain exactly constant in terms of the (real) numéraire. See also "Definition of the Numéraire" in chapter seven and "Price Indexes" in chapter twelve. □

practice it may be necessary to ignore the substitution possibilities in both production and consumption and to concentrate solely on the immediate (relative) reduction in the cost of consumption when making new estimates of shadow wage rates and of marginal social costs for nontradables.

In the second case the economy is thought to be moving rapidly toward a (relatively) free-trade policy. Assuming there are no sales taxes, market prices will then correspond to border prices so that there is no need to estimate a standard conversion factor. Now, however, the free-trade exchange rate must be estimated, which will depend on the elasticities of domestic supply of exports and domestic demand for imports—which in their turn will depend on substitution possibilities in production and consumption. As a first approximation, a convenient simple formula is:

$$(22) \quad \frac{\text{OER}}{\text{FTER}} = \frac{X\epsilon + M\eta}{X\epsilon\,(1 - t_x) + M\eta\,(1 + t_m)},$$

$$\begin{bmatrix} Official \\ exchange \\ rate \end{bmatrix} \div \begin{bmatrix} Free\ trade \\ exchange \\ rate \end{bmatrix} = \begin{bmatrix} Value\ of \\ imports\ and \\ exports\ in \\ free\ trade \end{bmatrix} \div \begin{bmatrix} Value\ of \\ imports\ and \\ exports\ in \\ free\ trade\ at \\ pre\text{-}free\text{-}trade \\ domestic\ prices \end{bmatrix}$$

where X is the f.o.b. value of exports and M is the c.i.f. value of imports under protection; ϵ is the elasticity of export supply and η is the elasticity of import demand; t_x is the average export tax (negative if it is a subsidy) and t_m is the average import tax (or the tax equivalent if quantitative restrictions are used); OER is the existing official exchange rate and FTER is the free trade exchange rate (per unit of foreign currency).

The movement to free trade will have a major impact on the economy and hence on shadow prices. Accounting prices of traded goods, properly deflated and expressed in terms of the real numéraire, will again tend to remain unchanged.[14] (Domestic market prices will rise or fall depending on whether the effects of trade liberalization [all $\beta = 1$] are more or less than offset by the devaluation.) The effect on the shadow prices of primary factors is less clear, however. For example, the downward effect of devaluation and upward effect of changes in β may, on balance, reduce or increase the shadow wage rate. Furthermore, the removal of distortion-inducing trade restrictions will cause previously protected sectors (whether traded or nontraded) to contract relative to previously nonprotected sectors (whether traded or nontraded). The ultimate

14. See note 13, above. □

Table 6. Sensitivity Analysis of the Ratio of the Official Exchange Rate to the Free Trade Exchange Rate

	Value of the ratio [a]			
When elasticity of foreign supply (ϵ) equals	*And when elasticity of foreign demand (η) equals*			
	1	*2*	*4*	*6*
1	0.85	0.82	0.80	0.79
2	0.88	0.85	0.82	0.81
4	0.91	0.88	0.85	0.83
6	0.92	0.90	0.87	0.85

a. The ratio is calculated for $t_m = 0.3$, $t_r = -0.05$, and $X = M$. See equation (22).

change in the shadow prices of primary factors—including the accounting rate of interest—will then also depend on the distribution of the efficiency gain between the various factors of production.

If it is expected with confidence that a free-trade policy will be implemented in the immediate future, considerable care should be taken in estimating both the FTER [15] and the likely effects on the prices of primary factors. Cruder methods will be appropriate if the intention is simply to test the effects of a free-trade policy if such a policy were to be implemented. Both t_m and t_x can be set equal to the ratio of total import duties to total imports and of total export taxes to total exports, respectively. If quantitative restrictions are used to restrain imports or exports, some attempt should be made to calculate tax equivalents. If the country is initially in balance-of-payments equilibrium, the only estimates required are for the elasticities and for M and X. Table 6 shows the sensitivity of the ratio of the OER to the FTER for different assumptions about the elasticities, assuming that $t_m = 0.3$, $t_x = -0.05$, and $X = M$. The table shows that the higher the elasticity of supply, ϵ, the higher the ratio OER/FTER, and that the higher the elasticity of demand, η, the lower the ratio.[16] In the event that no information is available on the elasticities, a reasonable approximation is to assume that the elasticities are the same so that they cancel from the formula.[17] As is apparent from

15. In particular, it may be necessary to allow for a less than perfectly elastic foreign demand for the country's exports. □

16. The result holds as long as $t_m > t_x$, which probably represents the typical case. □

17. The resulting formula is then very similar to that for the standard conversion factor discussed above. The formula developed in this paragraph, however,

the table, the ratio OER/FTER is not very sensitive to different assumptions about the elasticities. ☐

---

includes (in principle) the effects of quantitative restrictions and tariffs, whereas that for the standard conversion factor assumes that the quantitative restrictions will be retained and therefore excludes them. Moreover, the standard conversion factor allows for sales taxes, whereas the FTER allows only for trade tariffs and other restrictions. ☐

PART III

Estimation of Shadow Prices

VARIOUS WAYS OF ESTIMATING the shadow prices discussed in part II are considered in this part. As usual in applied economics, any method of estimation must be based on certain simplifying assumptions that may be more or less appropriate in any particular country. Because it is impossible to consider every conceivable eventuality, we have striven to make explicit the assumptions underlying the proposed estimating techniques. This should enable the analyst to judge, in the light of his special country knowledge, whether an estimation technique is justified and, if not, what alternatives may be more appropriate. The essential point is that the proposed methods of estimation should not be applied mechanically without first examining their relevance in the context of the specific country concerned. It should be apparent, however, that any refinement in the techniques can only be achieved at a cost, possibly in data collection and certainly in time. It is important, therefore, to weigh carefully the possible improvement in project selection wrought by a more refined estimate against the cost of that refinement.

The organization of part II is retained in presenting the material: in chapter ten the estimation techniques for the distribution weights (the ds, and v) are discussed, as well as those for the accounting rate of interest; in chapter eleven the shadow wage rate is examined; and in chapter twelve various methods of estimation for commodity prices, including the standard conversion factor, are put forward. At various points we suggest likely ranges for some of the parameters, based on available estimates and the experience of practitioners in this field. This should not be interpreted, however, as an attempt to impose rigid limits on particular parameter values but as a guide to the analyst. Although estimates lying outside the proposed range must be examined closely, such estimates should not be rejected out of hand. Whenever possible, analysts should present a range of likely parameter values as well as a best estimate. The range should not cover all possible values but only those which could occur with some reasonable degree of probability. The specification of such a range cannot be rigorous, but subsequent analyses will be better informed.

CHAPTER TEN

Distribution Weights

METHODS OF ESTIMATING a complete set of distribution weights for private consumption and private savings are described in this chapter. As discussed earlier, the weights for private consumption comprise two elements: d, the marginal value of nonaverage consumption (at domestic prices) in terms of the marginal value of average consumption, also at domestic prices; and v, the value of public income (measured in foreign exchange) in terms of the marginal value of average consumption at domestic prices.[1]

If the spread of the ds is large, projects that benefit the poor rather than the rich will be favored; if v is high, projects that save or generate public income will be favored. In light of stated government objectives and observed actions and policies, the analyst should formulate some preliminary views of, first, whether the government is seriously concerned with income distribution and, second, whether the government's revenue position is seriously constraining its actions. The first tells something about the spread of the ds: a government anxious to secure some redistribution of income through project selection will require the spread of the ds to be large, thereby favoring projects that benefit the poor; while the opposite holds for a government that is not so worried about redistribution. The second tells something about v: a government facing a severe shortage of public revenue will require v to be large, thereby favoring projects that save or generate public revenue; while the opposite holds for a government that can improve its revenue position fairly easily.

Statements of this kind are helpful in indicating the likely magnitude of the distribution weights and of v, although they do not provide precise numerical values. Before turning to the question of values, however, several caveats are in order. First, government actions and policies may be misleading guides and may often appear to contradict government statements: for example, government actions with regard to fiscal policy may often conflict with the government's stated objectives concerning

---

1. For a definition of symbols, see the glossary of symbols on page 149. □

income distribution. But inegalitarian fiscal measures may reflect constraints on fiscal policy rather than a lack of real commitment to objectives of income distribution.

Second, a severe shortage of public revenue does not necessarily imply
a high value of v: administrative bottlenecks may so reduce the effective-
ness of public expenditure that the funds would be worth more in the
hands of the private sector. It is clear from these two examples that, in
interpreting government actions or statements, the analyst should proceed
with caution.

DETERMINING THE dS

Choice of any one set of distribution weights involves value judgments
and therefore is not susceptible to objective estimation. In chapter seven [2]
we derived a set of distribution weights the egalitarian bias of which
could be summarized in one parameter, n. The relation between n and
the set of distribution weights relevant for marginal changes in consumption was shown in table 1.

Given that most governments employ some kind of progressive income
tax, it can be deduced that the value assigned by the government to increments in consumption decreases as the existing consumption level increases. Accordingly, it is possible to rule out $n=0$, which would imply
equal weights regardless of the existing consumption level. It is recommended, however, that all projects be appraised also at efficiency prices,
in which case, of course, $n=0$.[3]

As is shown in table 1, as n increases so the weight applied to any
particular consumption level below (above) the average consumption
level increases (decreases). For example, for an existing consumption
level of 25(300), $n=0.5$ implies a weight of 2(0.57); $n=1$, a weight of
4 or 2^2(0.33 or 0.57^2); and $n=2$, a weight of 16 or 4^2(0.11 or 0.33^2).
Thus, doubling n implies squaring the weight, so that small changes
in n can have fairly significant effects on the weight applicable to any
particular consumption level.

Now examine the change as the existing consumption level varies for a
given n. For example, with $n=1$, the weight on additional consumption
decreases proportionately with increases in the existing consumption
level: that is, for a consumption level y times as high (low) as some base
level, the weight is $1/y$ times as low (high) as that applicable to the base

2. See "Consumption Distribution Weight (d)" in chapter seven. □
3. See the final paragraphs of chapter six. □

consumption level. This may be considered quite a pronounced bias in favor of the poor in that the marginal consumption of a man four times as rich as another is only worth one-quarter of the value of consumption to the poor man. For $n=2$, the bias is even more pronounced, since the weight decreases with the square of the proportionate increase in the existing consumption level: that is, for a consumption level y times as high (low) as some base level, the weight is $(1/y)^2$ times as low (high) as that applicable to the base consumption level. Thus, the marginal consumption of a man four times as rich as another is worth only one-sixteenth of the value of consumption to the poor man. Alternatively, if $n=0.5$, the bias in favor of the poor is relatively mild, since the weight on additional consumption decreases proportionately with the square root of the proportionate increase in the existing consumption level: that is, for a consumption level y times as high (low) as some base level, the weight is $(1/y)^{1/2}$ times as (low) high as that applicable to the base consumption level. The marginal consumption of a man four times as rich as another is then worth one-half of the value of consumption to the poor man.

In principle, any value for n is conceivable; in practice, it probably makes sense to rule out extreme values and to consider a range for the likely value of n rather than to select a single value. Given the discussion in the previous two paragraphs the following procedure is recommended: first, as a preliminary step, set $n=1$ for all countries; and, second, as part of the sensitivity analysis, consider values of n ranging up to 1.5 (or possibly 2) for countries expressing a keen interest in redistribution and values ranging down to 0.5 for countries expressing only a mild interest in redistribution. This procedure has two advantages. First, all projects in all countries will be appraised for a value of n equal to unity, thereby facilitating international comparisons. Second, the analyst is not required to select a specific value for n but only to indicate the range in which the true value is likely to fall. The main disadvantage, of course, is that a project may have, for example, a positive net present value when n equals 1.5 and a negative net present value when n equals unity—or vice versa.[4] In such cases, the analyst would be required to decide whether n is closer to 1.5 than to unity—or vice versa—and the project would be accepted or rejected accordingly. But it is important that such a judgment—that, for example, n is closer to 1.5 than to unity in one particular project—be consistently applied to other projects in the same country. As more is learned about the influence of n on project selection (that is, as projects

4. See "Net Present Value and Economic Rate of Return" in chapter four. □

are rejected or accepted), it may be possible to narrow the range of likely values for this parameter.

ESTIMATE OF D

D, the summary distribution parameter,[5] depends on n, the elasticity of marginal utility with respect to consumption, and σ, the parameter of the Pareto cumulative distribution function. Given the range of values for n estimated in the manner described above, all that is needed to estimate D is an estimate of σ. Fortunately, σ is related to the Gini coefficient (a summary measure of inequality in income distribution).[6] The relationship is:

(23)   Gini coefficient $= 1/(2\sigma - 1)$.

The value of D can then be derived from table 3 in chapter seven or from equation (A15) in the appendix.

VALUE OF PUBLIC INCOME (v)

The value of public income, v, is one of the most difficult variables to estimate. Public income is expended for many different purposes, and to measure directly the value of some types of expenditure such as administration or defense is hardly possible. An omniscient and perfectly rational government would of course ensure that at the margin all types of expenditures were equally valuable, but obviously such an ideal is rarely if ever attained. Nevertheless, it may be a good working rule when deriving an estimate of v to proceed on the initial assumption of a perfect allocation of public resources.

Inasmuch as public investment is probably a major component of marginal public expenditure, it would seem important to attempt some estimate of its value—whether the assumption of a perfect allocation of public expenditure is accepted or not. In chapter seven and the appendix formulas are derived that may be used to obtain a preliminary estimate of the value of public investment.[7] The variables required for these formulas are q, the marginal product of capital in the public sector: that is, the net return earned by a marginal unit of public investment

5. See "Summary Distribution Measure (D)" in chapter seven. ☐
6. For information on Gini coefficients developed for many countries by the Development Research Center of the World Bank, see Shail Jain, *Size Distribution of Income: A Compilation of Data* (Washington, D.C.: World Bank, 1975). ☐
7. See "Value of Public Investment" in chapter seven and the concluding paragraph of "Derivation of v" in the appendix. ☐

(measured in foreign exchange) when all inputs and outputs are measured at efficiency prices (in foreign exchange); i, the consumption rate of interest; β, the ratio of the value of a marginal increase in consumption at shadow prices to its value at market prices for the average consumer; and s, the public sector's propensity to reinvest out of q.[8] All variables relate to the immediate future, the period five to ten years from the date of appraisal.

Provided $i > sq$, v can be estimated from the following formula:

$$(24) \quad v = \left[\frac{q - sq}{i - sq} \right] \Big/ \beta.$$

$$
\begin{bmatrix}
\textit{Value of the} \\
\textit{numéraire relative} \\
\textit{to private sector} \\
\textit{consumption at} \\
\textit{the average level}
\end{bmatrix}
=
\begin{bmatrix}
\textit{Marginal} \\
\textit{product} \\
\textit{of capital} \\
\textit{minus the} \\
\textit{rate of} \\
\textit{reinvestment}
\end{bmatrix}
\div
\begin{bmatrix}
\textit{Consumption} \\
\textit{rate of interest} \\
\textit{minus the} \\
\textit{rate of} \\
\textit{reinvestment}
\end{bmatrix}
\div
\begin{bmatrix}
\textit{Consumption} \\
\textit{conversion} \\
\textit{factor}
\end{bmatrix}
$$

The limitations of this estimate must be recognized. Two assumptions underlie the formula.

The first assumption is that all the variables—q, i, s, and β—remain constant over time, so that v also remains constant over time. This assumption generally implies that equation (24) overestimates v, because it may be reasonably expected that the divergence between q and i will decrease over time, thereby reducing the value of current investment. It may be sensible, therefore, to treat the value of v derived from equation (24) as a maximum estimate of its true value. In some cases, the maximum may not be very helpful. For example, if i is only slightly larger than sq, very high values can be obtained for v that prove quite sensitive to minor changes in i or sq. And if $i < sq$, the value of v tends to infinity, which is not a plausible result because it implies a zero value for consumption.[9]

The second assumption is that all project benefits augment either average private sector consumption or public investment. More realistically, the benefits will have a wider distribution, resulting in increases in consumption at many different consumption levels, increases in private savings and public current expenditure, and increases in public investment. It might be assumed that consumption benefits are distributed in the same way as is aggregate consumption, so that public investment

---

8. The formula in chapter seven is based on the assumption that $s = 0$, in which case $v = q/i\beta$. The more general formula shown here as equation (24) is derived in the appendix. □

9. See "Derivation of v" in the appendix. □

neither improves nor worsens income distribution. This assumption requires that equation (24) be multiplied by D, the summary distribution measure, but, given that D will often be close to unity, this may not be an important adjustment. A more important omission is the failure to allow for the possibility that some of the benefits may augment public current expenditure and private savings. Given the assumption that all public income is equally valuable and assuming that private savings are as valuable as public investment,[10] the simplest solution to the problem is to redefine $(1-s)$ as that proportion of q which is consumed in the private sector. This, however, raises two problems: first, it is extremely difficult to estimate this version of s[11] and, second, it increases the possibility that sq exceeds i, because the public sector's marginal propensity to reinvest out of q is only a fraction of the revised concept of s.

To offset the tendency to overestimate implicit in equation (24), a minimum estimate might be attempted by assuming that there is no reinvestment: that is, $s=0$. The formula then becomes:

$$(25) \quad v = \left[\frac{q}{i} \right] \Big/ \beta.$$

$$\begin{bmatrix} Value\ of\ the \\ num\acute{e}raire\ relative \\ to\ private\ sector \\ consumption\ at \\ the\ average\ level \end{bmatrix} = \begin{bmatrix} Marginal \\ product \\ of\ capital \end{bmatrix} \div \begin{bmatrix} Consump\text{-} \\ tion \\ rate\ of \\ interest \end{bmatrix} \div \begin{bmatrix} Consumption \\ conversion \\ factor \end{bmatrix}$$

Provided investment is considered more valuable than average consumption (that is, $v>1$), the elimination of reinvestment will reduce the value of v estimated from equation (25). Even this approach, however, could involve an overestimate of v if the assumed constancy of q and i over time (which constancy imparts an upward bias to v) has a greater influence than the elimination of reinvestment (which elimination imparts a downward bias to v). Given this caveat, it is nevertheless probably reasonable to treat equation (25) as a lower limit for the true value of v.

CRITICAL CONSUMPTION LEVEL

With a preliminary value—or range of values—computed for v, its plausibility should be checked by relating it to estimates of the critical

---

10. For the purpose of this general formula, it is probably reasonable to assume that private savings are as valuable as public investment; but, when the benefits of a specific project are being assessed, we recommend that a different value be used for private savings. See "Private Savings," below. □
11. See "Marginal Propensity to Reinvest (s)," below. □

consumption level. This is defined as the level of consumption at which the government is indifferent as between an increase in its own income (measured in foreign exchange) and the same quantity of foreign exchange assigned to private sector consumption. Symbolically, this requires computation of the consumption level at which $v=d/\beta$.[12] In other words, the ds, or n, having been determined previously, an estimate of v implies an estimate of the critical consumption level—and vice versa.[13]

This has two important consequences. First, it is possible to comment on the plausibility of estimates for v. For example, it would be reasonable to rule out estimates of v that imply a critical consumption level below some minimum (starvation) consumption level. Second, other government policies can be examined to shed further light on the critical consumption level and hence on v. The most obvious policy from this point of view is the payment of consumption subsidies (monetary or otherwise). One might reasonably presume that such payment indicates that the government places a higher value on the consumption of the subsidized consumers than on its own income. It follows that the point on the income scale at which consumption subsidies cease may be identified as the critical consumption level.[14] Subsidies, however, have administration costs and efficiency costs (the latter arising through a disincentive effect). In principle, allowance should be made for these costs, a circumstance that suggests that the true critical consumption level is below the point at which subsidies cease.

The general upshot of this discussion is that, in determining v, too heavy a reliance should not be placed on any single method of estimation. Ideally, an attempt should be made to assess the value of public expenditure in as many different directions as is possible and to draw conclusions only after due consideration of all available estimates.

USE OF CROSS-CHECKS

When judging the acceptability of these estimates, the analyst must keep in mind the overall objective of this part of the estimation process: to derive a set of ds and a value for v that provide the correct signals

12. Given that $d=(\bar{c}/c)^n$, for the critical consumption level (c^*): $d=(\bar{c}/c^*)^n=v\beta$, or $c^*=\bar{c}(v\beta)^{-1/n}$. □

13. Consumption can be defined only for a given set of market prices. Where rural and urban price differentials are large, we recommend the use of urban prices. See "Changes in Private Sector Income" in chapter eleven. □

14. As was noted just above, however, a unit of subsidy must be adjusted to reflect the foreign exchange cost of consumption by means of β. In particular, see note 12, above. □

for the selection of projects. Various formulas have been suggested that provide the theoretical rationale for the approach, as well as some assistance in estimation—*but use of the formulas should not be interpreted as binding constraints on the analyst.* The simplicity of the recommended formulas can lead to misleading results, especially in the case of v. For this reason we recommended a careful assessment of the critical consumption level. Equations (24) and (25) can help in setting the probable range for v; but, when considered independently, they can produce very implausible results. Similarly, it was possible to offer some advice on the appropriate value of n and hence the spread of the ds, but, again, if considered independently of other estimates, the advice could prove misleading. The critical consumption level, however, provides a useful, independent check on the plausibility of the value judgments underlying both the ds and v. We want to stress, however, that manipulation of the various formulas is no substitute for good judgment in arriving at convincing estimates of the ds and v.

To ensure the necessary crosscheck of the ds and v, we recommend the following procedure:

—First, make initial estimates of n and of the consumption rate of interest along the lines suggested in, respectively, the final paragraph of "Determining the ds," above, and "Consumption Rate of Interest," below.

—Second, estimate q, s, and β as explained, respectively, in "Marginal Product of Capital (q)" and "Marginal Propensity to Reinvest (s)," below, and "Conversion Factor for Consumption (β)" in chapter twelve.

—Third, use equations (24) and (25) to derive the probable range for v.

—Fourth, calculate the range of critical consumption levels implied by the above estimates of v, β, and ds.

—Fifth, estimate the critical consumption level independently, using the method outlined in "Critical Consumption Level," above.

—Sixth, if the independent estimate of the critical consumption level falls within the range derived from estimates of v, accept the initial value judgments.

—Seventh, if the independent estimate falls outside the range derived from estimates of v, adjust n, the consumption rate of interest, or both to change either the ds or the estimates of v.

It should be possible to derive a consistent, plausible, and fairly reliable set of weights through this iterative crosschecking.

ESTIMATING THE PARAMETERS OF v

As noted above, the preliminary estimate of v from the return to investment requires estimates of the four variables defined above.[15] Inasmuch as any project lasts for a number of years, these estimates should refer to the future values of the variables. Naturally, all projections are based to some extent on past behavior, but, where possible, important future developments that may affect the variables to be estimated should be allowed for. In particular, the estimates used in project appraisal should be consistent with those used in other areas of economic policy planning. In the following paragraphs we examine successively methods of estimating the consumption rate of interest, the marginal product of capital, and the reinvestment rate. The discussion of β is deferred.[16]

CONSUMPTION RATE OF INTEREST

The consumption rate of interest (CRI) was defined earlier as: CRI$=$ $ng+\rho$, where n equals the elasticity of marginal utility with respect to consumption; g equals the growth rate of per capita consumption; and ρ equals the rate of pure time preference. The CRI, which underlies the intertemporal weighting system, clearly involves value judgments, and as such it cannot be estimated objectively (except for g). The purpose of the CRI in project selection is to ensure that the government's preferences concerning future consumption (growth) and current consumption are adequately reflected in shadow prices. Countries that are heavily committed to growth should employ a low CRI, which will ensure that the future consumption benefits from today's investment are not heavily discounted. The ultimate effect is to make investment appear more attractive than current consumption, and, as can be seen from equations (24) and (25), the result is translated into shadow price terms by increasing the value of v.

Of the CRI's three component variables, n, g, and ρ, n has been discussed above.[17] An estimate of g may be derived from the growth rate estimates of gross national product, savings, and population available in national statistics offices. Consumption measured in money terms would of course have to be deflated by an appropriate consumer price index. With regard to ρ, we recommend fairly low values—say, 0 to 5 percent—on the grounds that most governments recognize their obligation to future

15. See "Value of Public Income (v)," above. □
16. See "Conversion Factor for Consumption (β)" in chapter twelve. □
17. See "Determining the ds," above. □

generations as well as to the present. (The possibility that future generations may be richer than the present generation is of course allowed for
by the presence of ng in the CRI formula. Pure time preference, ρ, is an
additional element.)

But because the CRI depends on both n and ρ, ρ should not be determined independently of n. For example, for a growth-conscious economy
that is also using a high value of n on (current) income distribution
grounds, to set $\rho = 0$ would ensure that the CRI is fairly low and hence
correctly reflect the government's growth objective despite the high value
for n. On the other hand, for a country that is more interested in current
consumption than in growth, but is not interested in income distribution
(implying a low n), to set $\rho = 5$ percent would ensure that the CRI is
fairly high and hence correctly reflects the government's preference for
current compared with future consumption despite the low value of n.
Intermediate values of ρ would be appropriate for countries that are not
interested in (current) income distribution (low n) but are interested in
growth (low CRI) or for countries that are interested in income distribution (high n) but not in growth (high CRI). In general, values for the
CRI ranging from 5 percent (for a country that is very growth con-
scious) to 10 percent (for a country that is more concerned with current
consumption) would not be unreasonable, but values outside this range
are possible.

MARGINAL PRODUCT OF CAPITAL (q)

The marginal product of capital in the public sector is the net return
earned by a marginal unit of public investment at border prices: that is,
when all inputs and outputs are measured at efficiency prices. Thus,
whereas the CRI indicates the social marginal rate of substitution between present and future consumption and is consequently a subjective
parameter, q indicates the marginal rate of transformation between present and future foreign exchange and is an objective parameter that in
principle can be observed. Two methods of estimation are described in
the following paragraphs: first, a procedure based on macro data, and,
second, one using micro data. Neither approach is particularly satisfactory.

As an upper limit for q, the ratio of incremental net output to capital
in the economy can be used; this is the inverse of the more conventional
ratio of incremental net capital to output, or ICOR. Given national data
on net investment and increases in net national product at constant
prices, the required ratio at least at constant market prices can be obtained immediately. Ideally, of course, the ratio should be measured at

border prices; this can be achieved by multiplying net output by a standard conversion factor [18] and multiplying net investment by a conversion factor for capital.[19] Denoting the resulting ratio by k, it can be concluded that k overestimates q for at least two reasons: first, k is an average concept, whereas q is a marginal concept; and, second, k neglects the contribution of other factors of production as well as that of technical progress.

A crude allowance can be made for labor's contribution by subtracting from k the ratio of the incremental national wage bill to investment on the grounds that the numerator of this ratio reflects labor's incremental (rather than marginal) product. As with k, this second ratio should also be estimated at constant market prices and then be adjusted to reflect border prices. The subtraction of this ratio from k provides an improved estimate of q. Ratios of incremental employment to capital can usually be derived from national statistics, but wage data are usually more difficult to obtain, especially for the informal and agricultural sectors. Because of this, it may be more productive to confine this approach to the modern sector of the economy: that is, to derive an estimate of k and hence q for the modern sector of the economy. Insufficient data on flows of sectoral investment may limit the applicability of this approach, but the analyst may find the relevant information in sector surveys, especially industrial.

Despite the adjustment for labor's contribution, the macro approach will probably still produce an overestimation of q, so it may be more fruitful to rely on micro estimates. Where available, pretax profits net of depreciation in the industrial sector will provide a useful base on which to estimate q. If this approach is adopted, the following points should be kept in mind. First, in regard to the return to all invested capital: if industry is financed by equity, medium-term borrowing, and long-term borrowing, a weighted average of the return to each type of investment is necessary, the weights being the proportion of total investment financed in each of the three ways. The relevant interest rates may be interpreted as the return on loan finance. Second, in regard to the real return: both the pretax profit rate and the interest rates should be deflated by the rate of inflation. Third, in regard to the return at border prices rather than at domestic prices: application of the appropriate conversion factors is the required adjustment. Fourth, if the observed variations about the average return are interpreted as random deviations from the true value, the

18. See "Standard Conversion Factor" in chapter twelve. □
19. See "Conversion Factor for Capital Goods" in chapter twelve. □

average value may be taken as the best estimate of the yield on capital in industry. In reality, deviations from this average may, of course, reflect monopoly power, risk differentials, and market fragmentation— and, even in the absence of such phenomena, the underlying data refer to average rather than marginal profits and relate to industry and not to the public sector.

As a final exercise, therefore, it might be useful to examine the economic return on recent World Bank and other projects as a guide to q In doing so, however, it might be necessary to make some adjustment to the estimated internal rates of return on these projects to ensure that they reflect efficiency rather than market prices.

MARGINAL PROPENSITY TO REINVEST (s)

We revised the concept of s to allow for public current expenditure and private savings out of q.[20] Given this revision, it is probably easier for estimation purposes to concentrate on $(1-s)$, the proportion of q that is consumed in the private sector. As with $q,$ we suggest the use of both macro and micro data. The macro approach is based on the assumption that both public and private investment have, on average, the same impact on private consumption. Given this assumption, it is possible to deduce the increment in private sector consumption at constant (border) prices as a proportion of the increment in gross national product at constant (border) prices in any year. An average over, say, five years based on national statistics office projections would be the most appropriate data source.[21] The weaknesses of this approach are immediately apparent. First, no allowance is made for changes in the fiscal system that could bias the estimate either upwards or downwards. Averaging over five years may, however, reduce the significance of this point—and, anyway, crude adjustments could be made for any major tax changes. Second, and more important, it might be anticipated that the increment in private sector consumption resulting from private investment is larger than that resulting from public investment, given that the financial profits of public investment accrue directly to the public sector. On the other hand, some public investment—which provides, for example, free social services— increases private sector consumption, and in most countries the profits of private investment are subject to taxation. Nevertheless, on balance,

20. See "Value of Public Income (v)," above. □
21. This effort should be carried out in conjunction with the estimate of q from macro data. □

it might be concluded that reliance on this method will result in an over-estimate of $(1-s)$ and hence an underestimate of s.

The alternative micro approach involves estimating the value of $(1-s)$ from a sample of public sector projects. The main difficulty with this approach is that $(1-s)$ will probably vary considerably depending on the type of project. Thus, $(1-s)$ might be very high for a road project because most of the benefits will accrue to the private sector, whereas an industrial project within the public sector might produce a low value for $(1-s)$. In principle, interest here lies in the value of $(1-s)$ for the "average marginal" project, which suggests the following procedure. From a selection of public sector projects covering the main investment sectors, compute the return to private sector consumption. This involves calculating the internal rate of return of each project if net benefits are redefined as the increase in private sector consumption at border prices for each year of the project's life. Increases in private sector income—and hence consumption—could appear on the benefit side of the original project (as, for example, reduction in transport costs) or on the cost side (increased wage payments). The specific values of $(1-s)$ obtained by expressing the estimated return as a proportion of the respective q for each project are then averaged, the weights being the proportion of total public investment devoted to the different types of project. This effort essentially involves a series of crude cost-benefit analyses (as does the estimate of q if project data are used) and is obviously time consuming. It offers, however, a potentially valuable cross-check on the value of s.

ACCOUNTING RATE OF INTEREST

The accounting rate of interest (ARI) is defined as the rate of fall in the value of the numéraire, which is public income measured in foreign exchange. It follows that, if at the margin a country is lending abroad, the real rate of return on foreign lending must represent a lower limit for the ARI because foreign lending is denominated in terms of the numéraire. Historical estimates of the marginal return from foreign lending on international markets suggest that this lower bound for the ARI is of the order of 4 percent in real terms.[22] Alternatively, if at the margin a country is borrowing from abroad, then the ARI should be at least equal to the marginal cost of such borrowing.[23]

22. See Deepak Lal, "The Return from Foreign Investment and the Lower Bound of the ARI" (World Bank, 1973; processed). ☐
23. See Garry Pursell, "Notes on a Shadow Discount Rate for the Ivory Coast" (World Bank, 1973; processed). ☐

In addition to these minimum estimates, another estimate of the ARI can also be derived by recalling that the ARI is that rate of discount which balances the supply of and demand for public investible resources. As such, the ARI should equal the internal social rate of return on the marginally acceptable project. In principle, this can be obtained only by an overall analysis of the investment budget, but, in practice, the following formula might be used as a rough guide to the true value of the ARI: $ARI = q - h$, where h adjusts for the distributional impact of public investment on private sector consumption.

We have already discussed q; [24] h may be derived as follows: given that s is the proportion of q that accrues to the public sector (and private sector savings), it follows that $(1 - s)q$ units of foreign exchange accrue to private sector consumption. If this increment augments the consumption of those at the average level of consumption, then:

$$h = (1 - s)q(1 - 1/v\beta) \text{ and}$$

$$(26) \quad ARI = sq + (1 - s)q/v\beta.$$

$$\begin{bmatrix} \text{Accounting} \\ \text{rate of} \\ \text{interest} \end{bmatrix} = \begin{bmatrix} \text{Rate} \\ \text{of} \\ \text{reinvestment} \end{bmatrix} + \begin{bmatrix} \text{Rate of consumption} \\ \text{generation in} \\ \text{terms of the numéraire} \end{bmatrix}$$

Given the particular formulation of the ARI in equation (26), it is obvious that the $ARI \gtreqless q$ depending on whether $1/v\beta \gtreqless 1$.

If the increment in consumption accrues primarily to the poor, however, the term $1/v\beta$ should be replaced by $d/v\beta$, where $d > 1$, which increases the probability that the $ARI > q$. The exact condition for this result is that on average all the increased consumption arising from public investment must accrue to people whose consumption is considered more valuable than public income. Because this requires that on average the increment in consumption must accrue to those below the critical consumption level, it is probably safe to conclude that the $ARI < q$, so that q may be regarded as a maximum estimate of the ARI. Finally, accepting that the consumption generated by public investment is less valuable than public income, it follows that the ARI decreases when s decreases. A minimum estimate for s has been derived; [25] this now enables us to interpret equation (26) as a lower bound for the ARI that may be above the lower bounds described earlier: that is, the return from (cost of) foreign lending (borrowing). Setting limits on the ARI in this fashion (that is, equation $[26] < ARI < q$) may be a more fruitful

24. See "Marginal Product of Capital (q)," above. □
25. See "Marginal Propensity to Reinvest (s)," above. □

approach than trying to derive a best estimate, since the limits suggested above may be sufficiently narrow for most appraisal purposes, especially if v is reasonably small, s is reasonably large, or both.

CHANGES IN v OVER TIME

The estimates—or range of estimates—obtained for the ARI in the above fashion should then be compared with those for the consumption rate of interest.[26] In the typical case, it might be expected that ARI≥ CRI, which result has certain consequences for the rate of change in v over time. In particular, if ARI>CRI, then v is declining over time, and if ARI=CRI, v is independent of time.[27] We therefore suggest the following procedure: First, if ARI≃CRI, treat v as a constant over the life of the project. Second, if ARI>CRI, calculate the project's net present value (NPV) on the assumption that v is time independent, and if NPV≥0, accept the project; if NPV<0, however, recalculate NPV on the assumption that v is falling at a rate equal to one-half of the difference between the ARI and CRI and accept the project if NPV≥0. The recommendations under the second point, above, are based on the relation between the rate of change of v and NPV and on the relation between the ARI, the CRI, and the rate of change of v. With regard to the first relation, NPV calculated on the (true) assumption that v is declining will always be equal to, or greater than, NPV, on the (false but convenient) assumption that v is time independent, because v appears in the denominator of the weight assigned to private sector consumption benefits. It follows that if, on the false assumption, NPV≥0, then it may also be deduced that the true NPV≥0.[28] With regard to the second relation, at any point of time the rate of change of v over time equals the difference between the ARI and the CRI.[29] But in addition, it might be expected that this difference between the ARI and the CRI would decline over time, so that the rate of fall of v would be declining over time.

Without a detailed model of the economy it is difficult to predict these changes, but as a reasonable practical solution it might not be too unrealistic to assume a rate of decline for v equal to one-half of the difference between the ARI and the CRI. If this procedure is adopted, however, it is recommended that the critical consumption level be recalculated on the basis of the assumed rate of fall in v for, say, ten to fifteen

26. See "Consumption Rate of Interest," above. □
27. See "Accounting Rate of Interest" in the appendix. □
28. This conclusion is reversed if CRI > ARI originally. □
29. See equation (A20) in the appendix. □

years in the future to see whether it still seems reasonable in the light of the independent estimate of the critical consumption level given the estimated rate of growth of average consumption.[30]

PRIVATE SAVINGS

For estimating v and the ARI, it has been assumed that private savings are as valuable as public income. This is probably a reasonable assumption for this purpose, given the level of accuracy at which an analyst is operating, but it may be important to have a more precise valuation of private savings when computing benefits for a particular project. We recommend the following procedure. As with direct taxes, we suggest that private saving be netted out of private sector income. Unlike taxes, however, private savings lead to future private income which should be costed, or valued, in the same way as any other increase in private sector income. In other words, private saving is initially assumed to be socially costless (that is, as valuable as public investment, or income), but then an adjustment is made to allow for the increase in future private sector income in excess of that generated by public investment.

We provide two examples to illustrate the above procedure. Consider first private saving that takes the form of lending to the public sector. This is similar to tax payments except that public borrowing involves debt servicing that will lead to future increases in private sector income. For example, if the entire annual debt repayment (b) per unit of private saving is consumed, the net cost of the consumption generated in any year is $b(\beta - d/v)/(1+\mu)^t$, where $(\beta - d/v)$ adjusts for the social costs and benefits of consumption and μ is the rate of inflation. Discounting by the ARI and summing over the life of the loan gives $b(\beta - d/v)/(r+\mu)$,[31] where r is the ARI. Alternatively, private sector saving may lead directly to private sector investment. In this case, assuming that private and public investment are equally efficient (that is, have the same q), the increase in future consumption (in excess of that generated by public investment) must be used in place of b. The return to private consumption from public investment is $(1-s)q$; thus, if the entire return from private investment is thought to accrue to private consumption, $b/(r+\mu)$ must be replaced by $sq/\beta r$, q already being expressed in constant border prices.

---

30. See "Critical Consumption Level," above. □
31. This is the sum of an infinite series. Given that most debt repayment schedules are finite, the expression employed in the text will overstate the true cost of consumption, assuming that $d/v < \beta$. □

Further refinements may be required in either formulation, especially if private savings represent a large portion of project benefits. For example, it may be desirable to allow for future savings out of the return from current savings or for profits tax.[32] For estimation purposes, the distribution weight d applicable to the consumption out of the return to savings might be set equal to the d applicable to the portion of the saver's income that is consumed in the initial period. The implicit assumption here is that the saver's consumption grows at the same rate as average consumption, so that d remains constant. Whatever approach is deemed appropriate in the context of the specific project, the ultimate objective is to obtain the net present social cost of the future private sector income per unit of current savings, this being the weight applicable to private savings. □

32. Compare "Value of Public Income (v)," above. □

CHAPTER ELEVEN

Shadow Wage Rates

IN ESTIMATING SHADOW WAGE RATES, it is necessary to consider three different types of cost that may occur when one extra man is employed on a project. These costs are: forgone marginal product, changes in consumption and savings, and changes in leisure. These three components of the shadow wage rate (SWR) were discussed at some length earlier,[1] so the emphasis here will be on particular estimation problems not considered in part II. Two general points should be stressed at the outset, however. First, the three components of the SWR—and hence the SWR itself—will differ between different types of labor, depending on such factors as skill, location, and season. Second, the three components of the SWR may not relate solely to the worker who is employed but, because of a migration effect or a change in wage rates, may affect other workers.

FORGONE MARGINAL PRODUCT

The standard procedure of estimating forgone output from market wage rates—as well as the limitations of the approach in situations in which the labor market does not operate efficiently—was described above.[2] Rather than repeat this discussion, we consider here two specific problems: that of estimating α, the accounting ratio to be applied to the market wage rate;[3] and that of incorporating migration effects into the SWR.

According to marginal productivity theory, labor will be hired up to the point at which its marginal value product equals the wage, the marginal value product being given by the marginal physical product times the output's market price to the producer. The social value of labor's marginal product is, of course, the marginal physical product times the output's shadow price—or, more conveniently, the marginal value product (that is, the market wage) multiplied by the ratio of the

1. See chapter eight. □
2. See "Forgone Output" in chapter eight. □
3. For a definition of symbols, see the glossary of symbols on page 149. □

shadow to the market price. For example, if the output is an exportable good subject to an infinitely elastic world demand, the appropriate shadow price for the output is its border price,[4] so that in this case α equals the ratio of the border price to the domestic producer price.

But more complicated cases can arise in which the marginal physical product comprises more than one type of output. In such an instance the simple ratio must be replaced by a weighted average of the accounting ratios for the different outputs, the weights being the proportion of the marginal value product accounted for by each type of output. In the absence of any specific information to the contrary, the standard conversion factor might be used as the appropriate accounting ratio. This, however, is only an approximation, in that the commodities on which the standard conversion factor is based may bear little correspondence to the commodities making up the marginal value product, and should therefore be used sparingly.

There is growing evidence to suggest that the creation of one job in the urban sector may induce more than one worker in the rural sector to migrate to the city. The economics of this migration effect presupposes that the urban wage is fixed, and that the labor market is adjusted by changes in the level of urban unemployment such that at the margin the potential migrant is indifferent as between the expectation of high-paying urban employment and the actuality of low-paying rural (under)employment. The essential feature of this equilibrating mechanism is that the rate of unemployment in the urban sector is unaffected by the creation of one new job, the number of responding migrants being exactly equal to the ratio of the total labor force (employed and unemployed) to total employment.[5] If this is the case, multiplication of one worker's marginal product by this ratio will provide the required value of forgone output.

CHANGES IN PRIVATE SECTOR INCOME

Workers on a project will often gain an increase in income, especially if the labor involved is drawn from the ranks of the rural un(der)-employed.[6] Here, we underscore several points that should be borne in mind when estimating such increases in income.

---

4. See "Tradables Subject to Infinite Elasticities" in chapter nine. □
5. For more information on the assumptions underlying such results, see Dipak Mazumdar, "The Rural-Urban Wage Gap, Migration, and the Shadow Wage" (World Bank, 1974; processed). □
6. See "Changes in Income" in chapter eight. □

First, the transfer of labor from the rural to the urban sector may involve an increase in both nominal income and in the cost of living. Unfortunately, any estimate of changes in real income runs into the usual index number problem in that the estimate will differ depending on whether the individual price differences are weighted by the rural or the urban consumption pattern.[7] The geometric mean is often used as an acceptable compromise price index, but, where breakdowns of consumption patterns are unavailable, it will probably be sufficiently accurate to inflate rural income by a rough estimate of the average difference between urban and rural price levels. In addition, it may be desirable to make some adjustments for such other considerations as free government services, on the one hand, and increased transport and adjustment costs for the worker, on the other. But whereas government services have both a resource cost and a private welfare benefit, transport and adjustment costs are not offset by an increase in private welfare. It may be appropriate, therefore, to add an extra component to the SWR formula to allow for such costs if they are thought to be significant.

Second, the increase in consumption may, of course, accrue to more than one worker. This is obvious if more than one worker migrates in response to the creation of one urban sector job. It is now necessary to consider not only the change in consumption of the worker who obtains the job but also the changes in consumption of the migrants who join the ranks of the urban unemployed or obtain casual employment in the informal sector of the urban labor market. Tracing through these effects is difficult, but, provided the number of workers migrating is small,[8] fairly rough estimates of the consumption change for the excess migrants will probably suffice. The consumption of more than one worker may also be affected through induced changes in wage rates. For example, assume that project demand for a particular type of labor is satisfied by an increase in the wage rate that releases labor from employment elsewhere. In this case, two consumption effects may be noted: first, there is a transfer of income from producers (or consumers) to labor equal to the increase in the wage rate times the number already employed; and, second, producers (or consumers) will now have more or less income available for expenditure on other commodities depending on

---

7. See M. FG. Scott, J. MacArthur, and D. M. G. Newbery, *Project Appraisal in Practice: The Little-Mirrlees Method Applied to Kenya* (London: Heinemann, forthcoming). ☐

8. See the final paragraph in "Forgone Marginal Product," above. ☐

whether the elasticity of demand for labor is greater than or less than unity.[9]

Third, in regard to the distribution of consumption increases and hence the identification of the relevant distribution weight: these weights, the ds, were defined for per capita consumption levels, c, in relation to average per capita consumption, $\bar{c}$. It follows that increases in consumption must also be expressed in per capita terms, which requires that allowance be made for the number of dependents supported by the worker. For example, if family income increases from w_1 to w_2, then, assuming equal sharing within the family, the distribution weight to be applied to the increase should be deduced from table 2 for values of $c_1 = w_1/N$ and $c_2 = w_2/N$, where N is family size. For any given pair of ws, the larger N, the higher the distribution weight, because the increased consumption is going to a greater number of individuals with lower per capita incomes than if N is smaller.

CHANGES IN LEISURE

Methods of evaluating changes in leisure were discussed earlier.[10] Here, we merely recommend that for purposes of sensitivity analysis, ϕ— the ratio of the social to the private evaluation of the disutility of effort— be set equal to its limits of zero and unity. □

9. This analysis duplicates that for the shadow price of a nontradable. See "Shadow Prices for Nontradables" in the appendix. □
10. See "Disutility of Effort" in chapter eight. □

CHAPTER TWELVE

Commodity Prices

FEASIBILITY STUDIES USUALLY CONTAIN estimates of commodity inputs and outputs either in volume terms or value terms. The social cost, or value, of these commodities may be obtained by multiplying the volume by the relevant shadow price or the value by the ratio of the shadow price to the relevant market price. We discuss, in order, methods of estimating shadow prices, first, for tradables with a fixed border price; second, tradables with a variable border price; and, third, nontradables. In addition, we examine various shortcuts that essentially involve using average border-to-market price ratios rather than commodity-specific ratios. In particular, we discuss conversion factors for consumption goods and capital goods and a standard conversion factor.

TRADABLES WITH FIXED BORDER PRICES

The appropriate shadow price for an imported good in perfectly elastic supply or for an exported good in perfectly elastic demand is the relevant c.i.f. or f.o.b. border price adjusted for transport and marketing margins.[1] For the major imported inputs, the feasibility study will often express costs in terms of c.i.f. prices, and, for the more important internationally traded commodities, estimates of f.o.b./c.i.f. prices at the major exporting-importing ports are available from national and international sources. Thus, there may often be a fairly firm data base for the major inputs and outputs of the project.

For other commodity inputs and outputs, less reliable methods may have to be adopted. Obtaining unit values for imports and exports from the trade statistics is one possibility, but usually the level of aggregation is insufficiently detailed or the reliability of value and volume figures is questionable. An alternative method involves computing the border price from the domestic price. For importables, for example, the c.i.f. price can be derived by subtracting (a) the relevant marketing margin (wholesale or retail), (b) the transport cost, and (c) the import tariff or sales

---

1. See "Tradables Subject to Infinite Elasticities" in chapter nine. □

tax (or both) from the domestic price. Conversely, for an exportable, the f.o.b. price can be derived by adding to the domestic price (a) the relevant marketing margin (wholesale or retail), (b) the transport cost, and (c) any export tariff or sales tax (or both). Marketing margins are available for some countries from surveys of distribution and tariff rates can be obtained from the country's customs tariff code.

The above account has not covered all eventualities: in any particular case it might be possible to use additional sources of information,[2] or additional complications might be encountered.[3] Procedurally, it will probably prove most convenient to keep the marketing margins separate and at the end of the process to convert them en bloc into shadow prices by means of an appropriate conversion factor.[4] It may also prove easier to attempt projections over time of border prices rather than to project domestic prices and convert them into border prices by means of the projected ratio between domestic and border prices.

TRADABLES WITH VARIABLE BORDER PRICES

For imported goods in less than perfectly elastic world supply or for exported goods in less than perfectly elastic world demand, the appropriate shadow price may, under certain circumstances,[5] be approximated by the marginal import cost or marginal export revenue.[6] Some of the major primary commodity exports from the less developed countries are likely to be subject to a less than infinitely elastic world demand, and such commodities, of course, are often the main output of a project. Estimates of the relevant elasticity of world demand for some of these primary commodities are prepared regularly by various national and international organizations, including the World Bank. It is important, however, to distinguish between the elasticity of demand for a particular commodity from a particular country and the elasticity of world demand for that commodity. Writing the former as η and the latter as η_w (both defined so as to be positive), the relation between the two is given by:

---

2. See Stephen Guisinger and Demetrios Papageorgiou, "The Selection of Appropriate Border Prices in Project Evaluation: Some Further Results," Economics of Industry Paper no. 3 (World Bank, 1973; processed). □

3. For example, a domestically produced version of an importable may be considered qualitatively inferior (superior) to the imported article. □

4. See "Marginal Social Cost," below. □

5. For which, see "Shadow Prices for Exportables" in the appendix. □

6. See "Tradables Subject to Finite Elasticities" in chapter nine. □

$$(27) \quad \eta = \frac{\eta_w + (1-a)\epsilon}{a},$$

$$
\begin{bmatrix}
\text{Elasticity of} \\
\text{foreign demand} \\
\text{facing a} \\
\text{particular} \\
\text{country}
\end{bmatrix}
=
\begin{bmatrix}
\text{Sum of elasticity of} \\
\text{total foreign demand} \\
\text{and elasticity of foreign} \\
\text{supply weighted by the} \\
\text{foreign share in} \\
\text{world exports}
\end{bmatrix}
\div
\begin{bmatrix}
\text{Domestic} \\
\text{share in} \\
\text{world exports}
\end{bmatrix}
$$

where a is the country's share in the world export market and ϵ the export supply elasticity of competing exporters.[7] Thus, the formula adjusts for the supply response of competing exporters: only if $a=1$ (that is, all exports are produced by one country) will $\eta = \eta_w$. In the absence of specific information on the supply response of competitors, a minimum estimate of η can be obtained by setting $\epsilon = 0$, so that η equals the world demand elasticity divided by the country's share in the world export market; η is then the relevant elasticity for computing marginal export revenue. International trade yearbooks provide data on export shares by commodities; but in calculating these shares, trade subject to bilateral agreements should be excluded.

In many cases, however, the use of marginal export revenue (or import costs) does not provide a good approximation to the true shadow price. More sophisticated estimates involve calculating domestic demand and supply elasticities.[8] If the exportable is an important part of domestic consumption, such as rice, some attempt should be made to estimate the domestic demand elasticity, information on which is often available from budget studies. If the export good is not consumed domestically, such as rubber, there is need only to estimate the domestic supply elasticity. Unless there is specific information on hand from a supply response study, it is recommended that fairly low values be used for the domestic supply elasticities,[9] in view of the fact that exports from most less developed countries are agriculturally based and may be subject to land constraints. Finally, equation (A23) in the appendix allows also for the income transfers occasioned by the change in price. Unless there is specific information to the contrary, it is recommended that the βs for producers and consumers be assumed equal and that the ds for producers and consumers be assumed equal and equated with D, the summary

7. For the definition of symbols, see the glossary of symbols. □
8. See equation (A23) in the appendix. □
9. See Bela Balassa, "Tariff Protection in Industrial Countries: An Evaluation," *Journal of Political Economy,* vol. 73, no. 6 (1965), pp. 573–96. □

distribution measure. The income transfer effect may then be written as $(1-a)(\beta-D/v)$, where a is the quantity consumed domestically expressed as a proportion of total domestic output. In some cases it may be important to allow for different distribution weights for consumers and producers, but the degree of refinement clearly must depend on both data availability and the sensitivity of the net present value to different assumptions about the commodity's shadow price.

NONTRADABLES

Equation (A24) in the appendix, the basic formula for the shadow price of a nontradable, comprises the marginal social cost (MSC) of an increase in supply and the forgone marginal social benefit (MSB) of a reduction in consumption elsewhere, including any income transfer effect. Provided the same assumptions are made as in the above paragraph—that is, that the βs for producers and consumers be assumed equal and the ds for producers and consumers be assumed equal—the income transfer effect is zero. This may often be an acceptable approach, but, where there is specific information about the respective income classes to which producers and consumers belong, different values should be used for the distribution weights.[10]

Whatever assumptions are made about the income transfers, information is needed also about the MSC, the MSB, and the elasticities of domestic supply and demand. With regard to the elasticities, it is recommended that, unless there is specific information to the contrary, an infinite elasticity of domestic supply be assumed. This assumption produces the simple result that shadow price equals MSC, there being no price change and hence no income transfers. Moreover, an infinitely elastic supply may be a reasonable assumption for most services that are usually labor intensive, as well as for some of the more capital-intensive nontradables such as electricity, especially if a relatively long time horizon (say, five years) is adopted.

For some nontradables, however, this assumption would be very misleading. In particular, some commodities may be in perfectly inelastic supply as a result of trade policies. For example, importables that are not produced domestically and that are subject to fully used quotas may be regarded as nontradables in perfectly inelastic supply, provided there is no reason to believe that the quota will be relaxed; the shadow price

10. The most important example of this is when production occurs in the public sector. □

in this case equals MSB. Methods of estimating MSC and MSB are described in the two sections following.

MARGINAL SOCIAL COST

In principle, the marginal social cost (MSC) of each nontraded input should be estimated by the decomposition method.[11] In practice, however, it is probably more convenient to compute the MSC—and hence the conversion factor—for representative examples of each of the major types of nontradable. The resulting conversion factors can then be applied directly to project-specific nontradable inputs. Conversion factors might usefully be estimated for such nontradables as electricity, retailing, wholesaling, construction, and transport. It should be borne in mind, however, that the conversion factors estimated in this fashion will be only approximate, in that the inputs of the representative examples need not correspond exactly to the inputs of the project-specific nontradable. If in a particular case this correspondence is thought to be especially weak, and if precision is important, the analyst should attempt a direct breakdown of the project-specific nontradable.

Decomposition of a nontradable into its constituent inputs to determine the MSC would ideally be accomplished through an input-output table, but use of existing or ad hoc industry studies and manufacturing and distribution censuses is also appropriate. In some cases only a crude analysis of inputs will be necessary.[12] As a first approximation the market value of the output net of corporate and business taxes (and of any excise tax included in the gross value of final output) could simply be deflated by the standard conversion factor;[13] to increase accuracy, the analyst could decompose for one round and then use the standard conversion factor for the remaining nontradable inputs; and for greatest accuracy, he could decompose completely, thereby avoiding the use of the standard conversion factor. A first-round decomposition into tradables, nontradables, and labor will give a useful insight into the likely magnitude of the MSC. The general approach essentially involves a cost-benefit analysis of the nontraded industry. If this is kept in mind, it should help in deciding which approximations are or are not acceptable. Both current and capital costs should be included in estimating the MSC.

11. See "Estimation of Marginal Social Cost" in chapter nine. □
12. In principle, the marginal input-output relations are being sought, but in practice the average relations will be sufficiently accurate. If constant returns prevail, then marginal and average coincide. □
13. See "Standard Conversion Factor," below. □

The latter may be converted into annuities that, when discounted by the accounting rate of interest over the capital's lifetime, have the same net present value as those capital inputs which they represent. The annuity may then be treated as a current input.

MARGINAL SOCIAL BENEFIT

From equation (A24) in the appendix, the ratio of the marginal social benefit (MSB) to the domestic price, p, may be written as:

$$(28) \quad \frac{MSB}{p} = \beta_1 + \frac{(\beta_2 - d_2/v) - (\beta_1 - d_1/v)}{\eta_d},$$

$$\begin{bmatrix} \text{Ratio of} \\ \text{marginal} \\ \text{social benefit} \\ \text{to market} \\ \text{price} \end{bmatrix} = \begin{bmatrix} \text{Consump-} \\ \text{tion} \\ \text{conversion} \\ \text{factor} \end{bmatrix} + \begin{bmatrix} \text{Net social cost of} \\ \text{income transfer} \\ \text{from consumers} \\ \text{to producers} \end{bmatrix} \div \begin{bmatrix} \text{Elasticity} \\ \text{of} \\ \text{domestic} \\ \text{demand} \end{bmatrix}$$

where β_1 (β_2) is the conversion factor for consumers' (producers') consumption; [14] d_1 (d_2) is the pure distribution weight assigned to consumers' (producers') consumption; v is the value of public income; and η_d is the elasticity of domestic demand.

It is apparent from equation (28) that if $\beta_2 - d_2/v = \beta_1 - d_1/v$ (that is, the redistribution has a zero net social cost or value) or if $\eta_d \to \infty$ (that is, there is no redistribution), then $MSB/p = \beta_1$.

In general, setting $MSB/p = \beta$ is recommended unless there is evidence to the contrary. The most important exception arises when demand is relatively inelastic and the nontradable in question is produced in the public sector. In this case, the following obtains:

$$(29) \quad \frac{MSB}{p} = \beta_1 - \frac{(\beta_1 - d_1/v)}{\eta_d};$$

$$\begin{bmatrix} \text{Ratio of} \\ \text{marginal} \\ \text{social benefit} \\ \text{to market} \\ \text{price} \end{bmatrix} = \begin{bmatrix} \text{Consumption} \\ \text{conversion} \\ \text{factor} \end{bmatrix} - \begin{bmatrix} \text{Net social cost} \\ \text{of decreased} \\ \text{consumer} \\ \text{income} \end{bmatrix} \div \begin{bmatrix} \text{Elasticity} \\ \text{of} \\ \text{domestic} \\ \text{demand} \end{bmatrix}$$

and if, further, $\eta_d \simeq 1$, then $MSB/p = d_1/v$, which is the social value of private sector consumption. Although this is a convenient simplification, where possible direct estimates of η_d should be used. Budget studies may provide information on this elasticity. If this approach is adopted, it may be appropriate to set $d_1 = D$, the summary distribution measure.

---

14. See "Conversion Factor for Consumption (β)," below. □

CONVERSION FACTOR FOR CONSUMPTION (β)

The consumption conversion factors (βs) are required to transform a marginal increase in consumer expenditure into its equivalent value at shadow prices: that is, the basket of commodities making up the consumer's marginal consumption pattern must be valued at shadow prices, and the resulting sum must be expressed as a proportion of the value of the same basket at market prices. In symbols, this is:

$$\beta = \sum_j a_j \lambda_j / p_j,$$

where $\sum a_j = 1$, a_j being the proportion of marginal expenditure devoted to the jth commodity; and p_j (λ_j) is the jth commodity's market (shadow) price. Of course, the a_j may differ for different consumers at the same income level, as well as for the same consumer at different income levels. In practice, however, it will probably prove sufficiently accurate to calculate different βs for urban and rural consumers and possibly for two or three different income groups.

Expenditure surveys provide the most detailed information on the a_j. To obtain the marginal consumption pattern, either the consumption patterns of consumers in different income groups can be subtracted or the identity between a_j and the product of the average propensity to consume the jth commodity and its expenditure elasticity can be used. In the absence of information on the consumption patterns of different income groups and on expenditure elasticities, the refinement of calculating different βs for different income groups probably will have to be forgone and resort made to a single consumption conversion factor. Failing this, reliance must be placed on informed estimates—or "guesstimates"—based on data from other countries for the proportions of exportables, importables, and nontradables in marginal expenditure—or use made of equation (3),[15] which requires only trade data on the value of the country's imports and exports of consumer goods. This latter approach is clearly only approximate, since the composition of trade in consumer goods need not correspond to the composition of domestic consumption. For example, coffee may bulk large in exports but may represent only a very small proportion of domestic consumption. Similar problems can arise on the import side if domestic production is the main source of supply for an importable such as rice that accounts for a large proportion of domestic consumption. With this in mind, ad hoc adjustments should be made in equation (3) on the basis of the "guesstimates" approach.

15. See "Derivation of β" in chapter seven. □

If a detailed breakdown of consumer expenditure is available, the shadow to market price ratios—that is, λ_j/p_j—should be estimated in the manner described in the earlier sections of this chapter. But if it is necessary to resort to the more approximate methods suggested above, average conversion factors are required for exportable, importable, and nontradable consumer goods. For exportables and importables, the average rate of tariffs or subsidies can be used. The average tariff rate on imports may be equated with the ratio of total revenues from import tariffs on consumer goods divided by the c.i.f. value of total imports of consumer goods. If this ratio is expressed as t_m, the λ_j/p_j appropriate for the proportion of marginal expenditure devoted to importables is $1/(1+t_m)$. An identical procedure can be used for exportables. If t_x is the ratio of total revenue from export duties on consumer goods divided by the f.o.b. value of total exports of consumer goods, the λ_j/p_j appropriate for the proportion of marginal expenditure devoted to exportables is $1/(1-t_x)$. For export subsidies, t_x is negative. The most convenient conversion factor for nontradable consumer goods is the standard conversion factor discussed below. It should be apparent that the use of such average conversion factors is itself an approximation that may not always be appropriate. In particular, it may be important to make some allowance for a less than perfectly elastic world demand for exports [16] and to allow for excise taxes levied on consumption goods.

CONVERSION FACTOR FOR CAPITAL GOODS

The conversion factor for capital goods performs the same service for capital goods that the consumption conversion factor provides for consumption goods. Inasmuch as this conversion factor is required only for estimating q, capital's marginal product, fairly crude methods will suffice. The following procedure is recommended:

—First, estimate the proportion of capital formation accounted for by construction and multiply the result by the conversion factor for construction.[17]

—Second, the remaining portion of capital formation will represent tradable (and probably imported) items of equipment, machinery, and vehicles.

—Third, estimate the average import tariff on such goods and hence their average conversion factor.[18]

16. See "Tradables with Variable Border Prices," above. □
17. See "Marginal Social Cost," above. □
18. Many countries admit capital goods duty free, in which case the average import tariff is zero and the average conversion factor is unity. □

—Fourth, multiply the results of the second and third steps, above.

—Fifth, the required conversion factor is then obtained by adding the results of the first and fourth steps, above.

STANDARD CONVERSION FACTOR

Although in general it is recommended that a different conversion factor be estimated for each nontradable, it is useful to have available a standard conversion factor (SCF) that can be used for minor nontradable inputs or for the nontraded goods remaining after one or two rounds of decomposition.[19] For this purpose, use might be made of the ratio of the value at border prices of all imports and exports to their value at domestic prices.[20] This is a generalization of the formula for β,[21] and as such is subject to the same limitations. An alternative approach involves estimating a set of conversion factors for as many commodities and services as possible, including the most important items in the economy (many of which will already have been estimated), and selecting the median of the resulting frequency distribution of conversion factors as the SCF. Whatever the method chosen, resort to the SCF should not be had unless there is reason to believe that any resulting error will be small in relation to the project's net present value.

TREATMENT OF QUOTAS

The treatment of quotas poses severe problems for the cost-benefit analyst. If a quota-restricted commodity is an important project input or output and the quota is fully used and rigidly applied, the commodity should be regarded as a nontradable and treated in the manner described in sections "Nontradables" through "Marginal Social Benefit," above. Many quotas are not fully used or are not rigidly applied, however, in which case it may be assumed that the commodity is fully tradable at the relevant border price. Such commodities should be regarded as untaxed tradables and treated in the manner described in the sections "Tradables with Fixed Border Prices" and "Tradables with Variable Border Prices," above. In a large number of cases between these two extremes the quota system does have some impact, in that domestic supply and demand are not allowed to adjust fully to border prices, but it is not rigidly applied. In this situation we recommend that the quota system be viewed as an imperfect substitute for a tariff system such that the observed difference

19. See "Marginal Social Cost," above. □
20. Commodities subject to fixed quotas should be treated as nontraded goods, provided that the quotas are already fully used and that they are not expected to be relaxed in the near future. □
21. See "Conversion Factor for Consumption (β)," above. □

between the border price and the domestic price may be treated as the equivalent tariff or subsidy; this implies that commodities falling in this category should be regarded as tradables subject to tariffs or subsidies and treated in the manner described in the two sections on tradables referred to above.

With regard to the standard conversion factor and other general conversion factors, the points made above may be applied directly to the treatment of quota-restricted commodities in the various estimating formulas. Because the general conversion factors are only approximate means of transforming bundles of commodities expressed in market prices into their equivalent value at shadow prices, it may be sufficiently accurate to treat all quota-restricted goods as though they are subject to tariffs, or subsidies, equal to the difference between the border and domestic prices. This approach, however, requires data on domestic-border price differences. Unfortunately, there is no simple method of arriving at these price differences: the only feasible method is direct observation. Nevertheless, the impact of quantitative restrictions is an important area for economic investigation and policymaking in general. It may be possible, therefore, to call on work performed in the context of national trade policy, especially in view of the proliferation of studies on effective protection, to supply information on the relevant price differences.

PRICE INDEXES

Price indexes have been mentioned earlier in two contexts: in reference to changes in the price level over time and to changes in the price level over space.[22] Here, we briefly review some of the issues to which these questions give rise. Since changes in the price level over space are comparatively simple, they are discussed first.

If the estimate of the critical consumption level—and hence the value of private consumption relative to public income—has been based on consumption levels measured at urban prices, benefits in the form of increased rural consumption must be inflated in order to make them comparable to public income. Conversely, if the critical consumption level has been based on consumption levels measured at rural prices, benefits in the form of increased urban consumption must be deflated. It is recommended that the appropriate price index be defined as the geometric mean of the weighted average of market price differences

22. See, respectively, "Definition of the Numéraire" in chapter seven, and "Dependence on Policy Assumptions" in chapter nine; and "Changes in Private Sector Income" in chapter eleven. □

when the weights are, first, the urban consumption pattern and, second, the rural consumption pattern. Similarly, to obtain the increase in real income, as perceived by a member of the private sector when he transfers from rural to urban areas, it is necessary to make allowance for the probable differences in the price level. In the event that breakdowns of urban and rural consumption are not available, approximations will be required. It might be possible, for example, to adopt an index based on a weighted average of price differences for the major consumption goods, the weights being determined in the light of the analyst's general perception of consumption patterns.[23]

In regard to changes in the price level over time, a price deflator is redundant in estimating shadow prices insofar as price projections and benefit and cost estimates have been made in real terms at market prices. Frequently, benefit and cost estimates are made in quantity terms, so that, to obtain estimates of benefits and costs at shadow prices, the simplest procedure is to project shadow prices and apply them directly to quantity estimates. In at least three instances, however, a price deflator is required: first, when devaluation causes changes in both absolute and relative shadow prices;[24] second, when benefits are approximated by revenues, as in public utility projects, and the prices are fixed in money terms; and, third, when statistics in current prices are being used to estimate shadow prices.

For such purposes, we recommend that the price index be based on the accounting value of the bundle of goods bought at the margin of expenditure by someone at the critical consumption level. The use of this index implies that the public income numéraire is required to have constant purchasing power at accounting prices over the bundle of goods defined above. This index may be computed directly by estimating changes in accounting prices over time or indirectly by estimating changes in market prices and accounting ratios over time.

In principle, the two methods yield the same result but in practice it may be convenient to adopt the indirect method to handle cases in which tariffs are fixed in money terms or in which estimates are based on current price statistics. In such cases it may often be sufficiently accurate to assume that the accounting ratios remain constant over time, so that it is necessary to deflate by a price index based on market prices only. To make this assumption in the event of devaluation, however, would not normally be appropriate. □

23. The foreign exchange cost of consumption, β, will depend, of course, on the location of the beneficiary if market prices are different in urban and rural areas. □
24. See "Dependence on Policy Assumptions" in chapter nine. □

APPENDIX

Technical Derivation of
Shadow Prices

A FAIRLY GENERAL DISCUSSION of the ideas underlying the derivation of shadow prices was presented in part II. The derivation itself, however, was not rigorous, the intention being to present an intuitively acceptable rationale of shadow pricing. Ideally, the complete set of shadow prices should be deduced from a fully specified model of the economy in which the various constraints are explicitly identified. The general equilibrium approach to shadow pricing has obvious conceptual advantages over partial equilibrium analysis, but the general equilibrium models amenable at present to analytical or numerical solution are fairly simple.[1] In this appendix the basic ideas are established in very general terms, but for the derivation of individual shadow prices a partial equilibrium analysis is used.

DERIVATION OF WEIGHTS

The welfare function assumes the following:

—First, that there are no consumption externalities (that is, the individual's utility is assumed to derive solely from his own consumption);
—Second, that the same utility function obtains for all individuals and displays diminishing marginal utility with respect to consumption; and
—Third, that total welfare in any period is the sum of the individual utility levels.

1. For examples of analytically and numerically soluble models, see, respectively, N. H. Stern, "Optimum Development in a Dual Economy," *Review of Economic Studies,* vol. 39 (2), no. 118 (1972), pp. 171–84; and C. R. Blitzer and A. S. Manne, "Employment, Income Distribution, and Shadow Prices in a Dualistic Economy" (World Bank, 1974; processed). □

Given these assumptions, welfare in period t may be expressed as:

$$(A1) \quad W_t = \int_0^{\bar{c}} U(c)f(c)dc,$$

where $U_c > 0$, $U_{cc} < 0$, $U(c)$ is the utility from consumption level c, and $f(c)$ is the density function of the distribution of consumption.[2] The government is assumed to maximize the following objective function:

$$(A2) \quad \text{Max } W = \int_0^\infty W_t e^{-\rho t} dt,$$

where $\rho \geq 0$ and is the rate of pure time preference.

SHADOW PRICES

The shadow price of the jth commodity or resource on any given development path in period $t = 1 (W_{j,1})$ is defined as:

$$(A3) \quad W_{j,1} = \Delta W / \Delta Q_{j,1}:$$

that is, the increase in welfare, ΔW, resulting from a marginal increase in the jth commodity or resource, $\Delta Q_{j,1}$. Typically, one commodity or resource is chosen as numéraire, and the shadow prices are then redefined relative to that numéraire. For example, if the Jth commodity is chosen as numéraire, the shadow prices may be defined relative to this numéraire as:

$$(A4) \quad \lambda_{j,1} = W_{j,1} / W_{J,1} \text{ and}$$
$$\lambda_{J,1} = 1.$$

General equilibrium analysis involves the simultaneous solution for all λ_j; in principle, this approach takes into account all changes in prices and incomes that are engendered by a marginal increase in the availability of any particular resource or commodity, given full specification of all the constraints and technological and behavioral relations. In practice, however, its value for actual project selection is severely circumscribed by the lack of detail and realism in the general models presently susceptible to economic analysis. The alternative approach, and the one adopted here, concentrates on the major price and income effects resulting from a marginal increase in any resource or commodity, but it stops short of a comprehensive coverage of all the general

---

2. For a definition of symbols, see the glossary of symbols on page 149. □

equilibrium effects on the grounds that the significance of the omitted effects is negligible.

NUMÉRAIRE

As numéraire—that is, the Jth commodity, or resource—public income measured in foreign exchange was chosen.[3] The choice of this numéraire permits the rewriting of the formula for a shadow price in the following fashion. For simplicity of exposition, assume that a marginal increase in the availability of the jth resource in period $t=1$ affects welfare only in period one,[4] so it is possible to drop the explicit reference to the time period and write:

$$(A5) \quad \lambda_j = \frac{\Delta W}{\Delta Q_j} \cdot \frac{1}{W_g},$$

where ΔW occurs in period $t=1$ and $W_g = W_{J,1}$, W_g being the notation adopted in part II. If it is assumed that the change in Q_j is sufficiently small that it does not alter W_g, and if H is defined as the change in utility levels in the private sector; that is: $H = \Delta W - \Delta Q_g W_g$, where ΔQ_g is the change in the quantity of the numéraire commodity or resource, then, setting $\Delta Q_j = 1$ by the choice of units:

$$(A6) \quad \lambda_j = \Delta Q_g + H/W_g,$$

which says that the shadow price equals the change in the numéraire commodity (public income measured in foreign exchange) plus any change in utility levels in the private sector measured relative to the chosen numéraire. Note that if an increase in the availability of any resource or commodity affects private sector consumption, the measure of ΔQ_g must allow for the increased demand for foreign exchange (the numéraire) required to satisfy this increase in private sector consumption. Thus, if $H \neq 0$ (that is, if utility levels in the private sector are altered), ΔQ_g will include not only the direct impact of the resource or commodity on foreign exchange but also the indirect effects resulting from changes in consumption patterns and levels.[5]

---

3. This is the numéraire used in I. M. D. Little and J. A. Mirrlees, *Project Appraisal and Planning for the Developing Countries* (London: Heinemann Educational Books, 1974). For an alternative formulation using aggregate consumption as numéraire, see United Nations Industrial Development Organization, *Guidelines for Project Evaluation* (New York: United Nations, 1972). □

4. This assumption is relaxed in "Derivation of v," below. □

5. In the terminology of part II, ΔQ_g corresponds to the sum of the efficiency price and βc, H/W_g corresponds to cd/v. See equation (8). □

The remainder of this appendix derives certain components of the shadow price formula presented as equation (6). In particular, the following sections through "Changes in d over Time" describe a method of systematically incorporating changes in utility levels—that is, H/W_g—into the shadow price formula by means of a set of distribution weights. The link between this set of weights and the discount rate required for project selection is derived in sections "Consumption Rate of Interest" through "Accounting Rate of Interest." The various threads of the argument are brought together in the concluding sections to derive shadow price formulas for traded and nontraded goods.

DISTRIBUTION WEIGHTS

If it is assumed that the increased availability of the jth commodity has only a marginal effect on one consumer's utility, W_c, then $H = W_c$. Defining:

$$d = W_c/W_{\bar{c}} = U_c/U_{\bar{c}} \text{ and}$$
(A7) $v = W_g/W_{\bar{c}},$

where $W_{\bar{c}}$ indicates the welfare value of consumption to someone at the average level of consumption, $\bar{c}$, the following is obtained:

(A8) $H/W_g = d/v.$

In other words, different increments in consumption will be compared relative to a consumption numéraire—that is, the marginal utility of consumption to someone at the average level of consumption—and then the consumption numéraire will be translated into public income measured in foreign exchange. The public income numéraire is v times as valuable as the consumption numéraire.

DERIVATION OF d

To determine the d weights, a utility function must be specified. The function usually selected has the property that the marginal utility of consumption has a constant elasticity, n, with respect to consumption at all levels of consumption. Thus, the following may be written:

(A9) $U_c = c^{-n},$

where $n > 0$ in order that marginal utility be nonincreasing. Total utility is obtained by integrating equation (A9); that is:

$$U(c) = \frac{c^{1-n}}{1-n} \text{ for } n \neq 1 \text{ and}$$

$$U(c) = \log_e c \text{ for } n = 1.$$

For infinitesimal changes in consumption, d is defined as:

(A10) $d = U_c / U_{\bar{c}} = (\bar{c}/c)^n$.

For nonmarginal changes in consumption, d is redefined as:

$$d = \frac{U(c_2) - U(c_1)}{U_{\bar{c}}(c_2 - c_1)},$$

where $c_2 > c_1$, which gives:

(A11)
$$d = \frac{\bar{c}^n (c_2^{1-n} - c_1^{1-n})}{(1-n)(c_2 - c_1)} \text{ for } n \neq 1 \text{ and}$$

$$d = \frac{\bar{c}(\log_e c_2 - \log_e c_1)}{(c_2 - c_1)} \text{ for } n = 1.[6]$$

The choice of an isoelastic utility function imparts to the weights certain properties that may conveniently be examined in relation to equation (A10). These properties are:

—The weight on consumption increments at all consumption levels is unity if $n = 0$;

—For $n > 0$,

$d > 1$ if $c < \bar{c}$, and also d increases as n increases,

and $d < 1$ if $c > \bar{c}$, and also d decreases as n increases;

—For any given $n > 0$, d depends only on the proportionality factor, $\bar{c}/c$, and is independent of the level of $\bar{c}$. This is called constant (relative) inequality aversion.[7]

DERIVATION OF D

Some effects of a project on the distribution of consumption may be difficult to trace, too small to bother about, or so general that all income classes may be affected. In principle, an analyst should evaluate the impact on each consumption class and integrate over the affected income classes; that is:

(A12) $H/W_{\bar{c}} = \left[\int_{c_0}^{\infty} U_c g(c) \, dc \right] / U_{\bar{c}},$

where c_0 is the minimum consumption level, and $g(c)$ describes the

---

6. Equations (A10) and (A11) were used to derive the numerical values for tables 1 and 2 in chapter seven. □

7. Increasing (relative) inequality aversion implies that d increases with c for given n. See M. S. Ahluwalia, "Distribution Weights, Utility Functions, and Project Analysis" (Washington: World Bank, 1973; processed). □

distribution of the increase in consumption across consumption classes. In practice, it might be possible to obtain specific information about $g(c)$, but, in the absence of such, an analyst might assume that the increase in consumption is distributed in the same way as current aggregate consumption, which implies that:

(A13) $g(c) = f(c)c/\bar{c}$,

where $f(c)$ is the density function of the distribution of aggregate consumption.

Assuming that consumption is distributed according to the Pareto function, for which the cumulative distribution function $F(c)$ is $1 - F(c) = (c_0/c)^\sigma$, the corresponding density function is given by:

(A14) $f(c) = F_c = \sigma c_0^\sigma c^{-\sigma-1}$.

Inserting equation (A14) into (A13) and the result into (A12) gives:

$$H/W_{\bar{c}} = D = \sigma c_0^\sigma c^{n-1} \int_{c_0}^{\infty} c^{-n-\sigma} dc.$$

Because for a Pareto distribution, provided $\sigma > 1$, $(\sigma-1)\bar{c} = \sigma c_0$, it is possible to write:

$$D = \sigma^n (\sigma-1)^{1-n} c_0^{n+\sigma-1} \left[\int_{c_0}^{\infty} c^{-n-\sigma} dc \right] \quad \text{or}$$

(A15) $D = \dfrac{\sigma^n (\sigma-1)^{1-n}}{(n+\sigma-1)}$,

which formula depends only on n, the elasticity of marginal utility with respect to consumption, and σ, the parameter of the Pareto function.[8]

In principle, it is possible to derive a more general formulation of D that allows for changes in distribution. Substitution of the isoelastic utility function and the Pareto density function into the expression for total welfare in any period (equation [A1]) gives:

(A16) $W/W_{\bar{c}} = \dfrac{\sigma c_0^\sigma \bar{c}^n}{1-n} \left[\int_{c_0}^{\infty} c^{-\sigma-n} dc \right] \quad \text{or}$

$$W/W_{\bar{c}} = \dfrac{\bar{c}(\sigma-1)^{1-n} \sigma^n}{(1-n)(n+\sigma-1)}.$$

---

8. Equation (A15) was used to derive the numerical values for table 3 in chapter seven. □

If both $\bar{c}$ and σ are allowed to vary, then:

$$dW/W_{\bar{c}} = \left[\frac{\partial W}{\partial \bar{c}} d\bar{c} + \frac{\partial W}{\partial \sigma} d\sigma \right] / W_{\bar{c}}.$$

The required welfare measure, D', is defined as $dW/d\bar{c}W_{\bar{c}}$. Because $\partial W/\partial \bar{c}W_{\bar{c}} = D$:

(A17) $\quad D'/D = 1 + \dfrac{n\bar{c}d\sigma/\sigma d\bar{c}}{(\sigma-1)(n+\sigma-1)}$,

where $\bar{c}d\sigma/\sigma d\bar{c}$ may be interpreted as the elasticity of σ with respect to $\bar{c}$; if this elasticity equals zero, $D'=D$.

CHANGES IN d OVER TIME

It should be apparent that the distribution weight, d, for any given increment in consumption may vary over time. For example, suppose an analyst wants to trace the time path of d for a given individual. Assuming that the difference in the growth rates of the average and the individual's consumption level is δ, for an infinitesimal change in consumption, the value of d in period t is:

(A18) $\quad d_t = \left(\dfrac{\bar{c}_t}{c_t} \right)^n = \left(\dfrac{\bar{c}_0 e^{\delta t}}{c_0} \right)^n = d_0 e^{\delta t n}$,

where the subscripts indicate time period. Clearly, if $\delta = 0$, then $d_t = d_0$ for all t. Alternatively, if $\delta > 0$, d_t increases over time, and if $\delta < 0$, d_t decreases over time. The weight for nonmarginal increments in consumption may also vary over time.

CONSUMPTION RATE OF INTEREST

Thus far, it has been shown how increments in consumption occurring at various consumption levels can be measured relative to the welfare value of an infinitesimal increment in consumption accruing at the average level of consumption. This can be done in each time period. But it may also be desirable to compare the value of consumption across time periods. Clearly, given a set of ds for each time period, it is necessary only to compare the marginal value of consumption at the average level across time periods to measure the present worth of any increment in consumption occurring at any consumption level and in any time period. Accordingly, the consumption rate of interest, CRI or i, is defined as the rate of fall over time in the value of the marginal utility of consumption at the average level of consumption.[9] Given the

9. It is possible in principle to define a consumption rate of interest (CRI) for

particular utility function, the welfare value, $W_{\bar{c}}$, of a marginal increment in consumption accruing at the average level of consumption in period t is:

$$W_{\bar{c}} = \bar{c}_t^{-n} e^{-\rho t},$$

where ρ is the rate of pure time preference. The consumption rate of interest is defined as:

$$\mathrm{CRI} = i = -\dot{W}_{\bar{c}}/W_{\bar{c}},$$

where the superior dot, $\dot{}$, indicates differentiation with respect to time, so that:

$$i = ng + \rho,$$

where g is the growth rate of average consumption.

DERIVATION OF v

v may be interpreted as the shadow price of public income expressed relative to a numéraire defined as the welfare value of a marginal increase in consumption accruing to someone at the average level of consumption; that is:

$$v = \Delta W / W_{\bar{c}} = \left[\int_0^\infty \Delta W_t e^{-\rho t} dt \right] / W_{\bar{c}}.$$

The precise derivation of v depends on the assumed economic environment. For example, it might be assumed that at the margin all public expenditure is either assigned to investment or to uses that are as socially valuable as investment. In this case, v may be interpreted as the shadow price (relative to the consumption numéraire) of both public income and public investment. It is possible then to proceed as follows. Assume that a unit of public income (measured in foreign exchange) assigned to investment produces an annual return net of depreciation of q. Assume that out of this return s is reinvested [10] and $(1-s)$ is

---

any consumption level. See Ahluwalia. *Distribution Weights.* In UN Industrial Development Organization, *Guidelines,* the CRI is defined as the rate of fall over time in the value of aggregate consumption, and in Little and Mirrlees, *Project Appraisal,* as the rate of fall over time in the value of employment-generated consumption. □

10. For simplicity, it is assumed that all reinvestment occurs in the public sector or that private saving is as valuable as public investment. More complicated formulations that distinguish between private and public reinvestment are described in UN Industrial Development Organization, *Guidelines.* □

assigned to private sector consumption either directly, through factor payments, or indirectly, through public current expenditure. It is now possible to derive v by summing the present value of the return in each period:

$$(A19) \quad v_0 = \sum_{t=0}^{\infty} (1-s_t) q_t G_t \prod_{t=1}^{t} (1+s_t q_t) / \prod_{t=0}^{t} (1+i_t),$$

where the subscripts indicate time periods, G_t is the value of a unit of nonreinvested benefits relative to the consumption numéraire, and Π indicates multiplication. Thus, in period t the capital stock, growing at a rate of $s_t q_t$, will equal:

$$\prod_{t=1}^{t} (1+s_t q_t);$$

that portion of the return which is not invested has a value in period t relative to the consumption numéraire of $(1-s_t) q_t G_t$ times the then existing capital stock; the present value of nonreinvested benefits in period t is obtained by application of the relevant discount factor, $\prod_{t=0}^{t} (1+i_t)$, where i_t is the CRI in period t; and finally, summation over all periods gives the required value for v_0.

Equation (A19) is still too general for estimation purposes,[11] but it does provide some useful insights. First, if $s_t q_t > i_t$ for all t (that is, if the growth rate of capital exceeds the discount rate), then $v_0 \rightarrow \infty$; alternatively, if $s_t q_t < i_t$, then the present value of future benefits will become very small as t increases, which ensures a finite value for v_0. Second, estimates of v tend to be very sensitive to the estimates of sq and i over time, especially if $s_t q_t \simeq i_t$ for all t. Third, if all the parameter values stay constant over time and $i > sq$, then, dropping the time subscript:

$$(A20) \quad v = \frac{(q-sq)G}{(i-sq)}.[12]$$

The implied constancy of v, however, has certain implications for the discount rate that are discussed in the following paragraph.

11. See "Value of Public Income (v)" in chapter ten. □

12. Equation (14) in chapter seven was derived from equation (A20) by setting $s=0$ and assuming that the entire return accrued at the average level of consumption, so that $G=1/\beta$, the β being required to obtain the increase in consumption at domestic prices made possible by an additional unit of foreign exchange. β is discussed further in "Derivation of β/MSC," below. □

ACCOUNTING RATE OF INTEREST

The discount rate is defined as the rate of fall over time in the value of the numéraire (public income measured in foreign exchange). From equation (A7):

$$\dot{v}/v = \dot{W}_g/\dot{W}_g - \dot{W}_{\bar{c}}/W_{\bar{c}}.$$

But the accounting rate of interest (ARI) equals $-\dot{W}_g/W_g$, and the consumption rate of interest (CRI) equals $-\dot{W}_{\bar{c}}/W_{\bar{c}}$, so that:

(A21) $-\dot{v}/v = r - i,$

where r = the ARI. It follows that if $r \neq i$, then v is changing over time and the use of equation (A20) to estimate v necessarily involves some degree of error. In particular, if $r > i$ (perhaps the typical case), v is declining over time and equation (A20) will overestimate v_0. Although equation (A21) is not useful in estimating the ARI, the ARI can be given a simple interpretation provided the assumption is accepted that at the margin all public expenditure is either assigned to investment or to uses that are as socially valuable as investment.[13] In this case the ARI is simply the internal social rate of return on the marginal public sector project, this being the discount rate that ensures a balance between the supply of and demand for public investable resources.

COMMODITY PRICES

The use of distribution weights can be illustrated by deriving some expressions for the shadow prices of commodities. The appropriate shadow prices for traded and nontraded goods can be examined in relation to a general formula that can be adjusted to fit specific cases. The only limitation on the formula is that it must be specified either for an exported or an imported item; whichever is chosen, the implications for a nontradable follow immediately. The formula for an exportable will be considered here because an analyst is more likely to encounter an exported good for which world demand is less than perfectly elastic than an imported good for which world supply is less than perfectly elastic. The derivation for an importable, however, is analogous.

Assume that a public sector project demands an exportable that is both produced and consumed in the private sector and for which world

---

13. This condition would be met, of course, if the government possessed perfect knowledge and acted rationally; that is, in a way consistent with the maximization of the specified welfare function. □

demand is less than perfectly elastic. The increase in demand will then lead to an increase in the border price, dp,[14] and an increase in private welfare given by:

(A22) $(-C-X+Q)\ dp$,[15]

where C is domestic consumption, X is exports, and Q is domestic production ($=X+C$). From left to right, there occur the loss in domestic consumer surplus ($C\ dp$), the loss in foreign consumer surplus ($X\ dp$), and the gain in domestic producer surplus ($Q\ dp$). To determine the change in social welfare these must be revalued relative to the numéraire (public income measured in foreign exchange). In the manner discussed above,[16] let d_1/v and d_2/v be the values assigned to domestic consumer and producer surplus, respectively, and assume that foreign consumer surplus is assigned a value of zero. Thus, the value of the gain in private welfare in terms of the numéraire is: $(d_2-ad_1)Q\ dp/v$,[17] where $a=C/Q$.

But any other repercussions of the price change must also be considered. There are at least four other effects.

First, the change in price may affect export earnings. If the elasticity of world demand is η_w, the increase in foreign exchange earnings is $(1-\eta_w)X\ dp$. Because this is already expressed in terms of the numéraire, it requires no further adjustment.

Second, the increase in price will increase or reduce domestic consumer expenditure on the exportable depending on whether the elasticity of domestic demand is less than or greater than one. Thus, depending on the value of the elasticity, consumer expenditure on other commodities will be either increased or reduced, and any change in consumer expenditure will have an impact on foreign exchange. If the elasticity of domestic demand is η_d, the increase in consumer expenditure on other commodities is $-(1-\eta_d)C\ dp$. To express this relative to the numéraire, it is multiplied by a weighted average of shadow to market price ratios, the weights being the proportion of the increased expenditure on other commodities devoted to each commodity. Let this weighted average be β_1, so that the change in consumer expenditure causes a reduction of $-(1-\eta_d)\beta_1 C\ dp$ in free foreign exchange, the chosen numéraire.

Third, the increase in producer expenditure will have a similar effect. If β_2 for producer expenditure is defined analogously to β_1, the increased

14. The border and domestic prices are assumed to be the same. □
15. This expression is only approximate for nonmarginal changes in price. □
16. See "Distribution Weights," above. □
17. This expression corresponds to H/W_g in equation (A6). For a more formal derivation, see "Distribution Weights and Price Changes," below. □

producer expenditure causes a reduction of $\beta_2 Q \, dp$ relative to the numéraire.

Fourth, finally, the cost of the increased domestic production must be considered. At domestic prices the increased production cost is $\epsilon Q \, dp$, where ϵ is the elasticity of domestic supply. To express this relative to the numéraire, it is multiplied by a weighted average of shadow to market price ratios, the weights being the proportion of increased costs attributable to each input. Let this weighted average be α, so that the increased production causes a reduction of $\alpha \epsilon Q \, dp$ in free foreign exchange (the numéraire).[18]

Thus far all the effects of the price change have been expressed relative to the numéraire so that they are directly additive. Because the increase in the value of demand at market prices is $(\eta_w X + \eta_d C + \epsilon Q) \, dp$, the ratio of the commodity's cost at shadow and market prices is given by:

$$(A23) \quad \frac{\epsilon\alpha - (1-a)(1-\eta_w) + a\eta_d\beta_1 + (\beta_2 - d_2/v) - a(\beta_1 - d_1/v)}{\epsilon + (1-a)\eta_w + a\eta_d}.$$

This general formula can be used to derive the shadow price for both exportables and nontradables.

SHADOW PRICES FOR EXPORTABLES

Equation (A23) is the appropriate shadow price formula for an exportable for which world demand is less than perfectly elastic. The last two terms of the numerator may be interpreted as income transfers between the public and private sectors. An increase in private sector consumption reduces public income measured in foreign exchange (hence the βs) but does increase welfare (hence the d/vs). If the βs $\simeq$ the d/vs, the net social cost of the income transfers is zero. If it is also assumed that domestic production is relatively inelastic (that is, $\epsilon \to 0$) and that domestic demand is relatively inelastic (that is, $\eta_d \to 0$) or is small compared with exports (that is, $a \to 0$), the ratio becomes $(1 - 1/\eta_w)$, which is the ratio of the marginal export revenue to the domestic price. Finally, if foreign demand is perfectly elastic (that is, $\eta_w \to \infty$), the ratio is unity, the border and domestic prices being equal by assumption.[19]

18. The summation of these four effects corresponds approximately to ΔQ_g in equation (A6). The correspondence is only approximate because the βs and the αs may contain elements that reflect changes in utility levels in the private sector and that should in principle be included in H/W_g. □

19. This analysis underlies the recommendations about the shadow price of

SHADOW PRICES FOR NONTRADABLES

If it is assumed that there are no exports (that is, $a=1$), the appropriate shadow price formula for a nontradable is obtained:

$$(A24) \quad \frac{\epsilon\alpha + \eta_d\beta_1 + (\beta_2 - d_2/v) - (\beta_1 - d_1/v)}{\epsilon + \eta_d}.$$

If supply is perfectly elastic (that is, $\epsilon \rightarrow \infty$), there is no change in price, and the ratio is simply α, the ratio of the marginal social cost (MSC) of production to the domestic price. Thus, given $\epsilon \rightarrow \infty$, the domestic price is the appropriate price for project analysis only if $\alpha = 1$. Alternatively, if supply is perfectly inelastic (that is, $\epsilon = 0$), the ratio may be interpreted as the marginal social benefit (MSB) of the output in the private sector divided by the market value of output. If, in addition, the βs = the $d/v s$, this ratio becomes β_1. Thus, given $\epsilon = 0$, the domestic price is the appropriate price for project analysis only if the income transfers cancel out and $\beta_1 = 1$.[20]

DISTRIBUTION WEIGHTS AND PRICE CHANGES

To derive a set of distribution weights to allow for price changes (rather than changes in consumption levels) the utility function, equation (A9), may be interpreted as an indirect utility function in which maximized utility is expressed as a function of total consumption expenditure, c, and prices.[21] For such functions, $U_p = -xU_c$, where U_p is the partial derivative of U with respect to the price, p, of a particular commodity, x is the quantity purchased of that commodity, and U_c the partial deriva-

---

tradables made in "Tradables Subject to Infinite Elasticities" and "Tradables Subject to Finite Elasticities" in chapter nine. □

20. This analysis underlies the recommendations in "Nontraded Commodities," "Estimation of Marginal Social Cost," and "Estimation of Marginal Social Benefit" in chapter nine about the shadow price for nontradables and importables subject to fully used quotas. □

21. For more information on indirect utility functions and their relationship to the more usual direct utility function, see L. J. Lau, "Duality and the Structure of Utility Functions," *Journal of Economic Theory*, vol. 1, no. 4 (1969), pp. 374–96. To include prices explicitly, equation (A9) should be rewritten to read:

$$U_c = c^{-n}\left[\prod_i \left(\frac{\gamma_i}{p_i}\right)^{\gamma_i}\right]^{1-n} \text{ for } n \neq 1 \text{ and } U_c = c^{-1} \text{ for } n = 1$$

where the γs are constants and p_i is the price of the ith commodity. $\prod_i$ denotes multiplication over i terms. This change does not affect the derivation of the $d s$ given in "Derivation of d," above. This form of the indirect utility function is consistent with a proportional expenditure system. □

tive of U with respect to consumption expenditure.[22] Relative to the consumption numéraire, $U_{\bar{c}}$, the welfare value of a price change is:

$$(A25) \quad U_p/U_{\bar{c}} = -xU_c/U_{\bar{c}}$$
$$= -xd,$$

where d is the distribution weight derived earlier.[23] Thus, equation (A25) formally justifies the use of d in analyzing the social value of marginal changes in prices.[24]

DERIVATION OF β/MSC

Inasmuch as the derivations of β and MSC (α) are essentially the same, only the former will be discussed here. β is required to transform the value of a marginal increase in consumption measured at domestic prices into its equivalent value relative to the chosen numéraire. If the increase in consumption comprises only one commodity, β will equal the ratio of the shadow to the market price for that commodity; for more than one commodity, β will be a weighted average of price ratios, the weights being the proportion of marginal expenditure devoted to each commodity. For example, if the market price of the jth commodity is p_j and the proportion of marginal expenditure devoted to the jth commodity is a_j, then:

$$\beta = \sum_j a_j \lambda_j / p_j,$$

where $\sum a_j = 1$ and λ_j is the shadow price of the jth commodity.[25] It should be clear that the a_j will be different for different consumers and will depend on both income elasticities and price elasticities if prices are changing. For α, the a_j should be defined as the proportion of increased costs attributable to each input.

SHADOW WAGE RATES

A shadow wage rate formula is not derived here because the actual derivation will depend crucially on the way in which the relevant labor

22. This result is independent of the form of the indirect utility function. See Lau, "Duality." □
23. See "Derivation of d," above. □
24. See "Commodity Prices," above. □
25. Note the similarity between β and the usual shadow exchange rate formulas. See "Dependence on Policy Assumptions" in chapter nine and M. FG. Scott, "How to Use and Estimate Shadow Exchange Rates," *Oxford Economic Papers,* vol. 26, no. 2 (July 1974), pp. 169–84. □

market works. In essence, the analyst is still working with equation (A24), but the distortions typically assumed to be present in the labor markets of less developed countries may warrant the introduction of additional considerations.[26]

26. See chapter eight and Deepak Lal, "Disutility of Effort, Migration, and the Shadow Wage Rate," *Oxford Economic Papers,* vol. 25, no. 1 (March 1973), pp. 112–26. □

Glossary of Symbols

Symbol	Definition

DISTRIBUTION WEIGHTS

ω Value of private sector consumption at consumption level c relative to the numéraire; $\omega = d/v$

d Value of private sector consumption at consumption level c relative to that at the average level of consumption; $d = W_c/W_{\bar{c}}$

v Value of the numéraire relative to private sector consumption at the average level of consumption; $v = W_g/W_{\bar{c}}$

W_c Marginal social value of private sector consumption at consumption level c

$W_{\bar{c}}$ Marginal social value of private sector consumption at the average level of consumption

W_g Marginal social value of foreign exchange in the public sector

D Summary distribution measure

G Value of a unit of nonreinvested benefits generated by investment

H Change in utility levels in the private sector resulting from a marginal change in the availability of the jth resource

$u(c)$ Utility at consumption level c

n Parameter of the utility function, that is, the elasticity of marginal utility with respect to consumption

γ Parameter of the indirect utility function

CONVERSION FACTORS

α Conversion factor for output

β Consumption conversion factor

M C.i.f. value of imports

X F.o.b. value of exports

t_m Average import tax

t_x Average export tax

η Demand elasticity defined so as to be positive [a]

ϵ Supply elasticity [a]

p Domestic price

λ Shadow price

a. η and ϵ may be further defined in context as, for example, elasticity of foreign demand or domestic supply. □

Symbol	*Definition*

GROWTH RATES AND INTEREST RATES

r	Accounting rate of interest (ARI)
q	Marginal product of capital at border prices
h	Distributional impact of marginally acceptable public sector project
k	Incremental capital to output ratio at border prices
i	Consumption rate of interest (CRI)
g	Growth rate of per capita consumption
ρ	Rate of pure time preference
μ	Rate of inflation
δ	Growth rate of average consumption minus growth rate of jth individual's consumption

SHADOW WAGE RATES

w	Market wage
m	Forgone marginal product at domestic prices
e	Ratio of the private value of forgone leisure to the market value of consumption
ϕ	Ratio of the social to the private evaluation of forgone leisure (or disutility of effort)

MISCELLANEOUS

S	Net social benefits
E	Net efficiency benefits
C	Private sector consumption
c	Consumption level
c^*	Critical consumption level
$\bar{c}$	Average level of consumption
$f(c)$	Density function of the distribution of consumption
$g(c)$	Distribution across consumption classes of a project-generated increase in consumption
$F(c)$	Cumulative function of the distribution of consumption
σ	Parameter of Pareto distribution function
Q	Output
x	Quantity consumed
N	Family size
a or a_j	Proportion (used in various contexts); $\Sigma a_j = 1$
b	Annual debt repayment per unit of private loan to the public sector
t	Time
s	Propensity of the public sector to reinvest out of q

Bibliography

The bibliography contains the reference cited in the text as well as some additional items of useful background reading. The basic ideas summarized in this book were first developed in the following books:

Little, I. M. D., and J. A. Mirrlees. *Project Appraisal and Planning for the Developing Countries.* London: Heinemann Educational Books, 1974. (This is a substantially revised version of Organization for Economic Cooperation and Development. *Manual of Industrial Project Analysis.* Paris: OECD, 1969.)

United Nations Industrial Development Organization. *Guidelines for Project Evaluation.* New York: United Nations, 1972.

Useful discussions of the above books are contained in the following studies:

Dasgupta, Partha. "A Comparative Analysis of the UNIDO Guidelines and the OECD Manual." *Bulletin of the Oxford University Institute of Economics and Statistics,* vol. 34, no. 1 (February 1972), pp. 33–52.

Lal, Deepak. *Methods of Project Analysis: A Review.* World Bank Staff Occasional Papers no. 16. Washington, D.C.: World Bank, 1974.

Joshi, Vijay. "The Rationale and Relevance of the Little-Mirrlees Criterion." *Bulletin of the Oxford University Institute of Economics and Statistics,* vol. 34, no. 1 (February 1972), pp. 3–32.

A more general discussion is provided in:

Layard, Richard, ed. *Cost-Benefit Analysis.* Penguin Modern Economics Readings, Hammondsworth, England: Penguin Books, 1972.

For a general equilibrium analysis of some of these ideas, see:

Blitzer, Charles R., and Alan S. Manne. "Employment, Income Distribution, and Shadow Prices in a Dualistic Economy." Processed. Washington, D.C.: World Bank, 1974.

Dasgupta, Partha, and Joseph E. Stiglitz. "Benefit-Cost Analysis and Trade Policies." *Journal of Political Economy,* vol. 82, no. 1 (January–February 1974), pp. 1–33.

Stern, N. H. "Optimum Development in a Dual Economy." *Review of Economic Studies,* vol. 39 (2), no. 118 (April 1972), pp. 171–84.

On particular shadow prices and related points, the following are recommended:

STANDARD CONVERSION FACTORS AND SHADOW EXCHANGE RATES

Bacha, Edmar, and Lance Taylor. "Foreign Exchange Shadow Prices: A Critical Review of Current Theories." *Quarterly Journal of Economics,* vol. 85, no. 2 (May 1971), pp. 197–224.

Balassa, Bela. "Estimating the Shadow Price of Foreign Exchange in Project Appraisal." *Oxford Economic Papers,* vol. 26, no. 2 (July 1974), pp. 147–68.

Scott, M. FG. "How to Use and Estimate Shadow Exchange Rates." *Oxford Economic Papers,* vol. 26, no. 2 (July 1974), pp. 169–84.

SHADOW WAGE RATES

Lal, Deepak. "Disutility of Effort, Migration and the Shadow Wage Rate." *Oxford Economic Papers,* vol. 25, no. 1 (March 1973), pp. 112–26.

Mazumdar, D. "The Rural-Urban Wage Gap, Migration, and the Shadow Wage." World Bank Staff Working Paper no. 197. Processed. Washington, D.C.: World Bank, 1974.

SHADOW INTEREST RATES

Blitzer, Charles R. "On the Social Rate of Discount and Price of Capital in Cost-Benefit Analysis." World Bank Staff Working Paper no. 144. Processed. Washington, D.C.: World Bank, 1972.

Lal, Deepak. "On Estimating Certain Inter-temporal Parameters for Project Analysis." Processed. Washington, D.C.: World Bank, 1973.

RISK AND UNCERTAINTY

Reutlinger, Shlomo. *Techniques for Project Appraisal under Uncertainty.* World Bank Staff Occasional Papers no. 10. Washington, D.C.: World Bank, 1970.

Pouliquen, Louis Y. *Risk Analysis in Project Appraisal.* World Bank Staff Occasional Papers no. 11. Washington, D.C.: World Bank, 1970.

On case studies, see:

Lal, Deepak. *Wells and Welfare.* Paris: Organization for Economic Cooperation and Development, 1972.

Scott, M. FG., J. MacArthur, and D. M. G. Newbery. *Project Appraisal in Practice, The Little-Mirrlees Method Applied to Kenya.* London: Heinemann, forthcoming.

Other references cited in the text are:

Ahluwalia, M. S. "Distribution Weights, Utility Functions, and Project Analysis." Processed. Washington, D.C.: World Bank, 1973.

Balassa, Bela. "Tariff Protection in Industrial Countries: An Evaluation." *Journal of Political Economy,* vol. 73, no. 6 (December 1965), pp. 573–94.

Guisinger, Stephen, and Demetrios Papageorgiou. "The Selection of Appropriate Border Prices in Project Evaluation: Some Further Results." Economics of Industry Division Paper no. 3. Processed. Washington, D.C.: World Bank, 1975.

Jain, Shail. *Size Distribution of Income: A Compilation of Data.* Washington, D.C.: World Bank, 1975.

Lal, Deepak. "The Return from Foreign Investment and the Lower Bound of the ARI." Processed. Washington, D.C.: World Bank, 1973.

Lau, L. J. "Duality and the Structure of Utility Functions." *Journal of Economic Theory,* vol. 1, no. 4 (December 1969), pp. 374–96.

Pursell, Garry. "Notes on a Shadow Discount Rate for the Ivory Coast." Processed. Washington, D.C.: World Bank, 1974.